Laura
Raynolds

Practicing Social Research

Practicing Social Research

Guided Activities to Accompany
THE PRACTICE OF SOCIAL RESEARCH
Sixth Edition

Sixth Edition

Theodore C. Wagenaar
Miami University
Oxford, Ohio

Earl Babbie

Wadsworth
Publishing
Company
Belmont, California
A Division of Wadsworth, Inc.

© 1992 by Wadsworth, Inc. All rights reserved. No part of this book may be reproduced, stored in a retrieval system, or transcribed, in any form or by any means, electronic, mechanical, photocopying, recording, or otherwise, without the prior written permission of the publisher, Wadsworth Publishing Company, Belmont, California 94002, a division of Wadsworth, Inc.

Printed in the United States of America

2 3 4 5 6 7 8 9 10—96 95 94 93 92

Contents

Preface

This book is designed for use in conjunction with *The Practice of Social Research*, sixth edition, by Earl R. Babbie. Its purpose is to reinforce and extend your understanding of the information in the text and to provide opportunities for you to apply the material in the textbook.

Each chapter begins with objectives, which focus your attention on the major points. They are specific statements of expected learning outcomes and will enhance your learning if you complete them. Glance through them before reading the chapter and refer to and complete them as you progress through the chapter. A summary of the chapter follows. Reading the summary before and after reading the chapter will give you both a preview and a review of the contents of the chapter.

A list of the key terms follows the summary. Mark each in the text and try to restate the definition in the text. Several of the definitions for these terms are presented in the matching exercise to give you some practice. The answers and page number references are contained in Appendix 2 for your convenience. The review questions test both knowledge and the ability to apply the concepts and principles presented in the text. Be sure to complete them and check your answers with the correct answers in Appendix 2. Page numbers are provided in the event you wish to determine why you answered a particular question incorrectly. Completing these questions will enhance your performance on exams.

The discussion questions encourage you to address several of the major issues raised in the chapter. Writing out the answers in your own words will strengthen your understanding and application of these issues.

The best way to learn research methods is through actual practice. Hence, we have included several short exercises for each chapter. Several of them involve you in analyzing data from the 1980 and 1990 General Social Surveys by using the Statistical Package for the Social Sciences. Before starting work on an exercise, we suggest you read through the entire exercise first so that you will know everything that is required. Reread those portions of the chapter that deal with the topics covered in the exercise. Then you should be ready to start work. In suggesting so many different exercises, it was our intention to provide you and your instructor with options. The exercises are all limited enough in scope that you will be able to complete many of them during the course. But we certainly did not intend for you to do them all. Make sure your instructor knows that. Instructors are reminded that suggested answers for many of the exercises are presented in the Instructor's Manual.

Special thanks go to Carol Kist for typing assistance and to Fred Halley for producing the data for Appendix 1.

We would be delighted to hear from you if you have any comments or suggestions for improving this book.

Part 1

An Introduction to Inquiry

Chapter 1

Human Inquiry and Science

OBJECTIVES

1. Define and illustrate agreement reality.

2. Define and illustrate experiential reality.

3. Identify the two criteria needed for scientists to accept the reality of something they have not personally experienced.

4. Differentiate epistemology from methodology.

5. Define and illustrate causal reasoning and probabilistic reasoning.

6. Differentiate the scientific approach from the native human inquiry approach to causal and probabilistic reasoning.

7. Differentiate prediction from understanding.

8. Describe the role of tradition and authority as sources of secondhand knowledge.

9. Define and illustrate each of the following errors in personal human inquiry: inaccurate observation, overgeneralization, selective observation, made-up information, ex post facto hypothesizing, illogical reasoning, ego involvement in understanding, premature closure of inquiry, and mystification.

10. Show how a scientific approach provides safeguards against each one of these errors.

11. Differentiate scientific inquiry from casual inquiry in two respects.

12. Describe what is meant by science being logico-empirical.

13. Describe the three major aspects of the overall scientific enterprise.

14. Define theory and indicate how it differs from philosophy or belief.

15. Give three examples of social regularities.

16. Respond to the three objections commonly raised regarding social regularities.

17. Define aggregate and present a rationale for why social scientists examine aggregates.

18. Give four examples of variables and their respective attributes.

19. Differentiate independent and dependent variables by definition and example, and show how they contribute to understanding causality.

SUMMARY

People live in a world of two realities. One is agreement reality, the things people consider to be real because they have been told they are real. The other is experiential reality, the things people know as a result of direct experience. The scientific approach to both realities demands that two criteria be met: an assertion must have both logical and empirical support. Hence science is a special form of human inquiry, the result of the human desire to predict future events and to understand patterns of cause and effect. The textbook will examine social science methodology, which is a subfield of epistemology (the science of knowing).

Native human inquiry is characterized by the recognition that some factors are caused by other factors, and that such patterns of cause and effect are probabilistic. Understanding native inquiry also means distinguishing prediction from understanding. While it is possible to predict a phenomenon without necessarily understanding it, understanding usually yields improved prediction abilities. In short, both what and why questions are addressed.

Two important sources of understanding are tradition and authority. The former involves accepting an inherited body of information and understanding, while the latter derives from the status of the transmitter of the knowledge. Authority and tradition can both assist and hinder human inquiry.

Personal human inquiry is prone to a number of errors. First, casual observation is frequently inaccurate. Science helps alleviate this error by mandating conscious observation. Second, people frequently overgeneralize on the basis of a few limited observations. Scientists protect themselves against overgeneralization by employing large random samples and by replicating studies. Third, people observe selectively, by paying attention to events that match a prior conclusion and ignoring those that do not. The scientific approach helps protect against this error by specifying in advance the number and types of observations to be made and by having several scientists investigate the same phenomenon.

A fourth error is made-up information: people make up information that would explain away a contradiction to a general conclusion. Science helps here by developing hypotheses that are tested and retested. The fifth error is ex post facto hypothesizing, which involves ignoring evidence that contradicts our conclusions and paying attention only to evidence that supports them. Scientists help avoid this error by gathering additional information. The sixth error is illogical reasoning, such as using an exception to prove a rule. Scientists avoid this pitfall by using systems of logic consciously and explicitly. Seventh, people sometimes fall victim to ego involvement in understanding. As a result, we may resist conclusions that make us look undesirable. The scientific norms of objectivity and intersubjectivity help prevent this error. Science can also prevent the premature closure of inquiry by maintaining that knowledge is cumulative and ever-changing. Finally, people sometimes attribute their inability to understand something to supernatural causes, known as mystification. But scientists believe that everything is potentially knowable and therefore continue to try and find answers to difficult questions. In short, scientific inquiry helps protect against all these errors by engaging in careful, conscious activity.

The scientific enterprise involves theory, research methods, and statistics. Research methods meet the scientific criterion of observation, theory meets the scientific criterion of logic or rationality by describing the logical relationships that exist among variables, and statistics help compare what is logically expected with what is actually observed. Theory addresses what is, not what should be. Hence scientists cannot settle debates on values. In short, social science can only help in knowing what is and why.

Social scientific theory and research help uncover the social regularities underlying social life. Some people argue that social regularities are sometimes trivial; scientists point out that common-sense understandings are often incorrect. Others argue that contradictory cases negate social regularities; scientists point out that social regularities represent probabilistic patterns that need not apply to every situation. Still others argue that individuals could upset a social regularity if they so desired; scientists point out that such action is possible but unlikely given the social norms that regulate social behavior. In short, social scientists analyze aggregates instead of individuals by examining the interrelationships among variables. They do so by examining the distributions of people across the attributes of the independent and dependent variables. Understanding causal connections remains paramount.

TERMS

1. aggregate
2. agreement reality
3. attributes
4. authority
5. causal reasoning
6. causation
7. description
8. ego involvement in understanding
9. empiricism
10. epistemology
11. ex post facto hypothesizing
12. experiential reality
13. explanation
14. inaccurate observation
15. independent variable
16. logic
17. made-up information
18. methodology
19. mystification
20. overgeneralization
21. prediction
22. premature closure of inquiry
23. probabilistic reasoning
24. relationship
25. selective observation
26. social regularities
27. theory
28. tradition
29. understanding
30. variables

MATCHING

___ 1. The science of finding out.

___ 2. A source of knowledge based on what we know simply by acquiring our culture.

___ 3. A source of knowledge that is obtained from experts.

___ 4. The assumption that a few similar events are evidence of a general pattern.

___ 5. Interpreting events to fit a general pattern that a researcher believes to be true.

___ 6. Logical and persistent patterns in social life.

___ 7. Logical groupings of attributes.

___ 8. An association that links variables.

REVIEW QUESTIONS

1. Most of what we know is a matter of
   a. personal experience
   b. a result of scientific discovery
   c. empirical evidence
   d. agreement reality
   e. logical support

2. Which one of the following is the best example of agreement reality?
   a. you meet 15 Graskinos and conclude that they are all prejudiced
   b. you develop a scale to measure love and give it to 20 people
   c. you accept prejudice as wrong because that is what the Bible says
   d. you do not get right next to people when you talk to them because it violates a norm
   e. you run an experiment to test the effect of crowding

3. The two foundations of science are
   a. tradition and observation
   b. observation and logic
   c. logic and theory
   d. theory and observation
   e. logic and generalization

4. When you hear the 4:27 train blow its whistle as you walk home from school every day, you can expect within minutes to smell Ms. Stockland's cooking. This is an example of
   a. understanding without prediction
   b. understanding with prediction
   c. prediction with understanding
   d. prediction without understanding
   e. scientific reasoning

5. "But my professor said that no significant differences exist between men and women regarding intelligence." What source of understanding does this example reflect?
   a. personal experience
   b. tradition
   c. authority
   d. public opinion
   e. science

6. A student meets two fraternity men at a party who talk about all the partying they do. She then concludes that all fraternity men party all the time. What error in understanding does this example reflect?
   a. inaccurate observation
   b. overgeneralization
   c. selective observation
   d. overemphasis on tradition
   e. overemphasis on authority

7. A researcher conducts a survey to test the hypothesis that women are more opposed to abortion than men are, and finds that men are more opposed than women. She then concludes that the respondents must have lied. This researcher has fallen prey to the error of
   a. inaccurate observation
   b. overgeneralization

c. selective observation
d. made-up information
e. illogical reasoning

8. You have just had a wonderful streak of great luck in your methods class: you've gotten A's on the last three tests and computer assignment. You have a research project due on the last day of class and you just know that you are going to flunk it. After all, something has to happen to break up this streak of good luck. You have fallen prey to the error of
a. illogical reasoning
b. ex post facto hypothesizing
c. mystification
d. made-up information
e. overgeneralization

9. Professor Black has developed what has come to be known as the "Black alienation scale." The scale has come under criticism from several scientists, and now Black is desperately trying to show why the criticisms are invalid and that the scale should be used. Black has fallen prey to the error of
a. inaccurate observation
b. selective observation
c. illogical reasoning
d. ego involvement in understanding
e. made-up information

10. Science
a. deals with what should be and *not* with what is
b. can settle debates on value
c. is exclusively descriptive
d. has to do with disproving philosophical beliefs
e. has to do with how things are and why

11. Scientists do not study individuals per se, but instead study social patterns reflecting
a. aggregates
b. collectivities
c. theories
d. attributes
e. norms

12. Professor Fremming examined the following categories of marital status: married, never married, widowed, separated, and divorced. These categories are known as
   a. variables
   b. attributes
   c. variable categories
   d. units of analysis
   e. theoretical elements

13. When social scientists study variables, they focus on
   a. attributes
   b. groups
   c. people
   d. characteristics
   e. relationships

14. Senator Josephson researched the effects of political orientation on attitudes toward abortion. "Political orientation" is an example of
   a. an attribute
   b. an independent variable
   c. an aggregate
   d. a unit of analysis
   e. a dependent variable

DISCUSSION QUESTIONS

1. How do tradition and authority hinder inquiry? How do they support it? Give examples.

2. Present both sides of the argument that the scientific approach is the best approach to understanding.

3. Explain why the errors in personal human inquiry that Babbie describes are so common.

EXERCISE 1.1

Each of us is confronted with decisions in our everyday lives that require that we gather and assess information on the different alternatives at hand and then make a decision. Examples of such decisions include the decision to attend college, buy a car or some other item, strike up a friendship with Person A or B, select a particular course, or take a trip to Point X or Y. You may have made an error in such decisions because your information was flawed by one or more of the errors of human inquiry that Babbie describes, or the decision may have been correct but for some of the wrong reasons. Recall and describe two decisions you have made that may have been flawed to some extent because information was based on one or more of the errors of human inquiry.

1. Describe each of the decisions.

2. Identify which of the errors of human inquiry as described by Babbie were involved in each decision.

3. Explain how a scientific approach may have helped prevent each error.

EXERCISE 1.2

List four social (not physical) regularities that are evident in day-to-day life. These could involve regularities in family life, friendship, large groups, work experiences, classroom activities, etc. Be sure you are describing social regularities.

EXERCISE 1.3

This chapter notes that variables and their attributes are at the heart of examining relationships in the social sciences. Key to formulating such relationships are independent and dependent variables.

Select two relationships, each involving an independent variable and a dependent variable. Clearly identify the attributes of each variable.

1. For your first relationship, identify the independent and dependent variables and describe the attributes of each.

2. For your second relationship, identify the independent and dependent variables and describe the attributes of each.

Chapter 2

Theory and Research

OBJECTIVES

1. Summarize the four motivations for doing social research.

2. List and define the three main elements in the traditional model of science.

3. Demonstrate how these three elements are linked in the scientific research process.

4. Define hypothesis and give three examples.

5. Differentiate inductive logic from deductive logic by definition and example.

6. Show how each of these approaches contributes to theory construction, both together and separately.

7. Define and show how each of the following terms is used in deductive theory construction: reality, objectivity and subjectivity, intersubjectivity, observation, fact, law, and theory.

8. Define and show how each of the following elements contributes to deductive theory construction: concepts, variables, and statements.

9. Describe the relevance of paradigms.

10. Identify the major tenets of the three major social scientific paradigms.

11. Outline and illustrate the basic steps in theory construction.

12. Explain how grounded theory reflects the inductive approach to theory construction and give an example.

13. Summarize the results of the Wells and Picou study regarding the connection between theory and research.

SUMMARY

Chapter 1 showed how scientific inquiry is a product of both logic and observation. This chapter formalizes that analysis by examining the respective roles of theory and research. The close link between the two is again demonstrated.

Social scientists do research for four basic reasons. First, they desire to test formal theories. Logical reasoning enables them to expand and modify theories. Second, they explore unstructured interests, often without clearly established relationships and variables at the outset. The purpose is to clarify the relevant variables and relationships. Third, social scientists engage in applied research to help answer policy questions. Fourth, they perform involuntary research in order to promote their careers. Students also engage in involuntary research as part of methods courses.

There are three main elements in the traditional model of science: theory, operationalization, and observation. Theory provides a backdrop for clarifying possible relationships among variables. Operationalization enables the measurement of variables so that their relationships can be empirically examined. Observation involves the actual collection of data to test the hypothesized relationships (hypotheses). This entire strategy is also known as hypothesis testing.

Theory construction proceeds through deductive logic and/or inductive logic. With deductive logic, scientists progress from general principles and theories to specific cases; with inductive logic, they proceed from particular cases to general theories. In reality, theory and research interact through a symbiotic interchange of both deduction and induction.

Social scientists employ several elements in constructing deductive theories. They assume that reality exists and is knowable, although they differentiate a subjective approach from an objective approach. Objectivity is enhanced through intersubjectivity, whereby multiple investigators study the same topic. Observation refers to the information gathering required to study aspects of reality. Social scientists agree that a fact means some phenomenon that has been observed, and that a law reflects a universal generalization about a class of facts.

Theories contain three basic elements. Concepts are the basic building blocks of theories and are abstract elements representing classes of phenomena within a given field of study. Operationalized concepts are known as variables, while statements portray the relationships among concepts. There are several types of statements: principles are universal generalizations, axioms are basic assertions assumed to be true, propositions are conclusions drawn about the relationships among concepts, and hypotheses specify expectations about empirical reality.

The statements that make up a theory must be systematically organized in some logical structure. For example, the concepts should reflect real-world phenomena, the statements should be causal, and the entire theory should contribute to understanding. Theories are frequently the product of paradigms, which are fundamental models for organizing our understanding of reality. Paradigms assist scientists in identifying problems as well as strategies for examining such problems. Three major paradigms exist in the social sciences. The interactionist paradigm stresses the interactions among individuals and the interpretations that participants ascribe to such interactions. The functionalist paradigm stresses the components of any social system and how those components are interrelated by the functions that they perform. The conflict paradigm stresses persistent conflict at all levels of social interaction.

Theory construction follows these major steps: (1) specify the topic of interest, (2) specify the range of phenomena the theory addresses, (3) identify and specify the major concepts and variables, (4) determine what is known about the hypothesized relationships, and (5) reason logically from the propositions obtained in the preceding steps to the specific topic under analysis.

In contrast to the deductive approach, the inductive approach to theory construction strives to uncover patterns based on actual observation; this approach is also known as grounded theory. This approach is seen most often in field research, although it can be used in other designs as well. Grounded theorists argue that the inductive approach is superior to deductive theorizing because the social scientist does not enter the field with preconceived theoretical constraints.

Social scientists link theory and research in a variety of ways. Wells and Picou documented the many different uses of theory, and found that only one-fourth of the articles examined involved testing theoretically derived hypotheses. They also found a substantial increase in the use of theory over the last half decade, and found a particular increase in the use of the traditional hypothesis-testing model.

TERMS

1. concepts
2. conflict paradigm
3. deductive logic
4. fact
5. functionalist paradigm
6. hypothesis
7. hypothesis testing
8. inductive logic
9. interactionist paradigm
10. intersubjectivity
11. law
12. objectivity
13. observation
14. operationalization
15. paradigm
16. proposition
17. reality
18. statements
19. subjectivity
20. theory
21. variable

MATCHING

_____ 1. The specification of the steps, procedures, or operations followed to actually measure variables.

_____ 2. Reasoning from particular instances to general laws.

_____ 3. Reasoning from general laws to particular instances.

_____ 4. Abstract elements representing classes of phenomena within a field of study; the building blocks of theory.

_____ 5. A class of attributes.

_____ 6. A conclusion drawn about the relationships among concepts, based on the logical interrelationships among axioms.

_____ 7. A fundamental model or scheme that organizes our view of something.

_____ 8. The paradigm that focuses on how the components of society are interrelated.

REVIEW QUESTIONS

1. Professor Haas developed an interest in the role of company picnics in maintaining an organization's culture. Because little work has been done, she attended several picnics, took lots of notes on what was going on, and developed some research questions. Which motivation for research is exemplified?
   a. test formal theories
   b. explore unstructured interests
   c. perform applied research
   d. perform involuntary research
   e. perform evaluation research

2. The three main elements of the traditional model of science are
   a. theory, operationalization, experimentation
   b. operationalization, hypothesis testing, theory
   c. observation, experimentation, operationalization
   d. theory, observation, hypothesis testing
   e. experimentation, hypothesis testing, theory

3. Which of the following is the **best** example of a hypothesis?
   a. the greater the level of education, the greater the tolerance for alternative lifestyles
   b. socialization in childhood has a significant impact on adolescent sex-role identity
   c. there are more female than male college students
   d. religiosity equals frequency of church attendance and praying
   e. actions are based on perceived costs and rewards

4. Which one of the following approaches to scientific reasoning does Babbie support?

a. primarily deductive
b. primarily inductive
c. both inductive and deductive
d. primarily syllogistic
e. both syllogistic and logical

5. Professor Pellson noticed that the students who sat in the front row in her classes usually got A's. Soon she decided that students who sit in the front row are generally good students. This is an example of
   a. deductive reasoning
   b. inductive reasoning
   c. probabilistic reasoning
   d. causal reasoning
   e. deterministic reasoning

6. Babbie reviews Wallace's model for portraying science. A particularly significant feature of this model shows that science
   a. generally begins with theories
   b. generally begins with hypotheses
   c. generally begins with observations
   d. generally begins with empirical observations
   e. can begin at any of these points

7. Social scientists have found that the following conclusion is universal across settings: as the size of a group increases, its complexity increases. This reflects a
   a. law
   b. theory
   c. concept
   d. paradigm
   e. hypothesis

8. The statement "Barb is a better computer programmer than Cathy" is which kind of statement?
   a. objective
   b. observed
   c. intersubjective
   d. subjective
   e. factual

9. The U.S. Government wishes to spend $1 billion on the unemployment problem. Twelve researchers, unknown to each other, are hired to use essentially the same procedures to see if they come up with the same results. Which characteristic of science is reflected in this example?
   a. intersubjectivity
   b. specificity
   c. generalization
   d. determinism
   e. logico-empiricism

10. Professor Waits began her study of the effects of high school course work on math anxiety by clearly stating certain basic assumptions upon which her theory is based. Which of the following did she use?
    a. propositions
    b. principles
    c. paradigms
    d. hypotheses
    e. axioms

11. The paradigm that accounts for the impact of economic conditions on family structures is the
    a. interactionist paradigm
    b. functionalist paradigm
    c. systems paradigm
    d. conflict paradigm
    e. exchange theory paradigm

12. Which of the following is *not* an element in deductive theory construction?
    a. specification of topic
    b. identification of major concepts and variables
    c. assembly of propositions about the relationships among those variables
    d. logically reasoning from those propositions to the specific topic one is examining
    e. all are elements

13. Professor Todd observes playground interaction for a month to develop a theory that accounts for the problems observed. This is an example of
    a. deductive theorizing
    b. grounded theory
    c. conceptualization

d. ex post facto hypothesizing
e. paradigm estimation

14. Which of the following is *false* regarding the research on how sociologists use theory in their research?
a. the use of theory has increased
b. the vast majority of researchers use theory to develop testable hypotheses
c. the use of the traditional hypothesis-testing model has increased
d. of those using theory to test hypotheses, most get results that support the hypotheses
e. all are true

DISCUSSION QUESTIONS

1. Figure 2-1 in the text (page 49) portrays the traditional image of science. Describe that model, being certain to discuss the role of the three main elements: theory, operationalization, and observation.

2. Describe how the elements of deductive theory construction fit together. Be specific.

3. Contrast deductive and inductive logic. Describe specific research issues that are appropriate for each and explain why.

4. Show how theory and research are closely linked. Indicate what each contributes to the other.

EXERCISE 2.1

A major focus of this chapter is the difference between deductive and inductive logic. Your assignment is to develop studies using each approach.

DEDUCTIVE LOGIC

1. Identify a topic of interest. You might select religiosity, feminism, or occupational success if you cannot identify a topic.

2. Explain what your theory will address. It might be factors promoting religiosity, why some people are more feminist than others, or why some people are more successful in their occupations than others.

3. Specify the range of phenomena your theory addresses. All people? Women only? Americans only?

4. Identify and specify your major concepts and variables.

5. Derive at least one specific testable hypothesis, such as: younger females are more likely to be feminist than older females. Be sure your hypothesis reflects a specific relationship between two variables.

INDUCTIVE LOGIC

1. Select one of the following "observations" or select one of your own. If you select one of your own, make sure it is very specific.
   a.   women like coed dorms more than men do
   b.   students prefer male instructors over female instructors
   c.   older people are more likely to vote Republican than are younger people
   d.   your own:

2. Describe the specific behaviors or statements made by people that might lead to the observation you selected.

3. Based on the discussions and examples in the chapter, derive (make up) a reasonable theory for your observation. It should be more general than your observation.

EXERCISE 2.2

Babbie describes the major social scientific paradigms. Identify the major paradigms in one of the other disciplines (e.g., history, psychology, political science, economics) you have encountered in college. Explain your choice of discipline and paradigms.

EXERCISE 2.3

Imagine that you are a social scientist who wishes to examine in greater detail the implications of the paradigms discussed by Babbie. Specifically, you wish to apply the conflict and the functionalist paradigms in a study of how your university works. Give examples of how each paradigm may affect what you examine in your study.

Chapter 3

The Nature of Causation

OBJECTIVES

1. Describe the deterministic model of behavior and show why this model is important for social scientific inquiry.

2. List three factors that are **not** part of the deterministic model.

3. Contrast the idiographic and the nomothetic models of explanation by definition and example.

4. Determine which of these two models is more probabilistic and which model is more dehumanizing, and explain why.

5. List and illustrate the three prerequisites for establishing causality.

6. Differentiate a necessary cause from a sufficient cause by definition and example.

7. Define and illustrate each of the following errors of reasoning: provincialism, hasty conclusion, questionable cause, suppressed evidence, and false dilemma.

8. List in proper order the five steps underlying the scientific method, and summarize each step.

9. Summarize the two basic problems that prevent the easy application of this traditional model.

10. Document how interchangeability of indexes helps resolve these two problems.

SUMMARY

Determinism lies at the base of a causal approach to understanding in social science. Determinism means that all social phenomena are the result of prior causes and that these causes themselves are the product of prior causes. This deterministic perspective contrasts with a freewill image of human behavior in which social phenomena are the product of personal decisions. This freewill image causes many people discomfort in dealing with the realities of determinism. However, social scientists do not believe all human actions and thoughts are determined. Neither do they believe that causal patterns are simple. Hence, social scientists employ probabilistic causal models.

Social scientists use two models of explanation to account for human behavior. The idiographic model lists all the specific prior events and conditions that influence a given behavior, and is frequently employed by historians. Social scientists typically employ a model by which they discover the most important factors causing a given type of behavior or attitude, which is known as the nomothetic model of explanation. This model helps identify general patterns of cause and effect and is probabilistic in its approach. Some people think that following this model dehumanizes the individual person, who has individual reasons for behaviors and attitudes.

Three requirements must be met in order to establish causality. First, the cause must precede the effect in time. Second, the two variables must be empirically related. Third, the observed empirical relationship should not be the result of the effects of some third variable on each of the two original variables. Compromises must be made in applying these prerequisites. For example, a perfect correlation is not a criterion of causality. Neither does the approach mandate the identification of variables that are simultaneously necessary and sufficient; either situation can be the basis for making causal assertions. A necessary cause involves something that must generally be present for the effect to follow, and a sufficient cause involves something that, if present, generally guarantees the effect.

Errors in causal reasoning will confront you often. Field research is particularly prone to several logical errors. Provincialism exists when the researcher interprets people's behavior from a particular point of view. Hasty conclusions emerge when insufficient evidence is available. Researchers may overlook additional causes in their quest to identify an immediate cause. They may also intentionally or unintentionally suppress evidence that contradicts their conclusions. Finally, false dilemmas are constructed when researchers believe that selecting one cause necessitates ruling out all other causes. The scientific method helps detect such errors.

The traditional view of the scientific method involves a clearly specified set of time-ordered procedures: theory construction, derivation of hypotheses, operationalization of concepts, collection of empirical data, and empirical testing of hypotheses. This model does not correspond completely with the way research actually occurs. For example, empirical relationships between variables are seldom perfect. In short, measurement and association are tightly linked.

Social scientists employ the interchangeability of indexes to deal with the problems of measurement and association. Multiple indicators are used for a given variable. Using this strategy, a theoretical hypothesis is accepted as a general proposition if it is confirmed by all of the separate indicators. If only certain indicators apply, then the scientist has specified the conditions under which the relationship holds.

TERMS

1. association
2. determinism
3. false dilemma
4. general proposition
5. hasty conclusion
6. idiographic model of explanation
7. interchangeability of indexes
8. necessary cause
9. nomothetic model of explanation
10. probabilistic
11. provincialism
12. questionable cause
13. sufficient cause
14. suppressed evidence
15. traditional deductive model

MATCHING

_____ 1. A theoretical hypothesis that has been confirmed by all empirical tests.

_____ 2. A relationship between two variables.

_____ 3. The property that allows scientists to make the same conclusions concerning the relationship between two variables when different indicators are used to define the variables.

_____ 4. The perspective that assumes that behavior is the product of forces and factors in the world beyond the individual's control.

_____ 5. The model of explanation that aims at the enumeration of the many considerations that lie behind a given action.

_____ 6. The model of explanation that aims to discover those considerations that are most important in explaining general classes of actions and events.

_____ 7. The condition that must be present for the effect to follow.

_____ 8. A condition that, if present, inevitably results in an effect.

REVIEW QUESTIONS

1. Which one of the following is *not* part of the deterministic nature of scientific explanation?
   a. all events have causes
   b. most events have only one cause
   c. scientists do not know the causes of all events
   d. not all causes operate the same way in different situations or with different people
   e. all are included

2. Which one of the following *best* reflects the idiographic model of explanation?
   a. Professor Guys wishes to explain alienation with causal variables
   b. Professor Owings wishes to identify all or almost all the reasons why people retire early

c. Professor Rumpler wishes to perform an exploratory study of doctor-nurse interactions

d. Professor Wong wishes to identify the major causes of religiosity

e. Professor Hamill wishes to extend the generalizability of his grounded theory analysis of death anxiety

3. Which of the following *best* reflects the nomothetic model of explanation?
   a. Professor Guys wishes to explain alienation with causal variables
   b. Professor Owings wishes to identify all or almost all the reasons why people retire early
   c. Professor Rumpler wishes to perform an exploratory study of doctor-nurse interactions
   d. Professor Wong wishes to identify the major causes of religiosity
   e. Professor Hamill wishes to extend the generalizability of his grounded theory analysis of death anxiety

4. Which one of the following is *true* regarding the idiographic and nomothetic models of explanation?
   a. the idiographic model is both more dehumanizing and more probabilistic than the nomothetic model
   b. both models are dehumanizing and equally probabilistic
   c. both models are dehumanizing, but the nomothetic model is more probabilistic
   d. both models are dehumanizing, but the idiographic model is more probabilistic
   e. the nomothetic model is more dehumanizing but less probabilistic than the idiographic model

5. Which one of the following hypotheses *best* fits the three criteria of causality?
   a. an increase in status attainment causes an increase in age
   b. an increase in educational attainment causes an increase in status attainment in occupation, controlling for several variables
   c. an increase in drowning causes an increase in ice cream consumption
   d. an increase in conservatism causes a religious conversion, controlling for several variables
   e. more males than females frequent bars

6. Which one(s) of the following is/are *true*?
   a. smoking is a necessary and sufficient cause of lung cancer
   b. socioeconomic status is a necessary and sufficient cause of GPA

c. a high GPA is a necessary and sufficient cause for occupational success
d. all are true
e. none are true

7. The traditional deductive model begins with
   a. theory construction
   b. operationalization of concepts
   c. empirical testing of hypotheses
   d. derivation of theoretical hypotheses
   e. collection of empirical data

8. When attempting to implement the traditional deductive model of research, two basic problems that occur are
   a. operationalization is rarely unambiguous, and collection of empirical data is problematic
   b. empirical associations are never perfect and collection of empirical data is problematic
   c. theory is often unrelated to empirical reality, and empirical associations are almost never perfect
   d. operationalization is rarely unambiguous, and theory is often unrelated to empirical reality
   e. operationalization is rarely unambiguous and empirical

9. Professor Flint examined the relationship between happiness and income. If he used interchangeability of indexes, which of the following would he do?
   a. examine how income is related to various measures of happiness
   b. examine how various researchers have measured happiness
   c. examine the various theories for explaining happiness
   d. examine the various approaches for measuring the reliability of the happiness measure
   e. examine the various approaches for measuring the validity of the happiness measure

10. The basic implication of interchangeability of indexes is that
    a. the nomothetic model of explanation is superior to the idiographic model
    b. social scientists have difficulty determining their measures
    c. measurement makes little sense outside the empirical and theoretical contexts of the associations to be tested

    d.   it should be used to help reduce the possible alternatives for measuring a concept

    e.   causality is extremely difficult to assess in the social sciences

11. The *main* goal of scientific research is
    a.   prediction
    b.   understanding
    c.   theory construction
    d.   hypothesis testing
    e.   to provide data for policy decisions

12. Professor Warshay did an observation of why students attend college. He developed a typology of four reasons. His typology helps support a theory he is developing and confirms his personal beliefs about why students attend college. Because of his biases, he has difficulty seeing other possible reasons. Which logical error is he committing?
    a.   questionable cause
    b.   suppressed evidence
    c.   false dilemma
    d.   hasty conclusion
    e.   provincialism

DISCUSSION QUESTIONS

1. Explain why people are uncomfortable applying the nomothetic model, and determinism in general, to human behavior and attitudes. Then present your views along with reasons for your views.

2. Explain why causes that are both necessary and sufficient are difficult to identify in the social sciences.

3. Explain why Babbie states that it is incorrect to view the process of measuring variables as distinct from the process of determining the associations among variables.

EXERCISE 3.1

A key focus of this chapter is determinism—identifying factors (independent variables) that affect other factors (dependent variables). Your assignment is to practice identifying these variables.

1. Identify a dependent variable—some event, behavior, or attitude that varies from time to time and whose variation you wish to explain.

2. Identify an independent variable whose variation you believe might explain variation in the dependent variable you described above.

3. State a causal hypothesis for your independent and dependent variables.

4. Discuss what criteria need to be satisfied before you can reasonably argue that there is a causal relationship between your two variables. In your discussion, note any alternative arguments or factors that should be examined before accepting your causal hypothesis. Apply these alternative factors to your specific hypothesis.

EXERCISE 3.2

Select one of the attitudinal variables listed in Appendix 1 of this workbook. Explain how this issue would be examined within the idiographic and the nomothetic models of explanation. You might even use other variables noted in the appendix. Be specific.

EXERCISE 3.3

Identify three examples of cause-and-effect relationships in everyday life that may have reasonable alternative explanations. For example, education causes greater tolerance of alternative viewpoints. Provide one or two possible alternative explanations for your three examples. In the example, simply growing older (instead of going to college) may cause greater tolerance. Explain what might be done in a study to see whether these alternatives are viable. That is, briefly design a study that would enable you to determine which of the causes is the most important.

Part 2

The Structuring of Inquiry

Chapter 4

Research Design

OBJECTIVES

1. Identify the two major aspects of research design.

2. Define and illustrate the three basic purposes of research.

3. List three reasons for performing exploratory studies.

4. Define units of analysis and identify and illustrate each of the basic types.

5. Define and illustrate the ecological fallacy.

6. Define and illustrate reductionism.

7. Define and illustrate the three points of focus for research.

8. Select four possible research issues, and identify both the unit of analysis and topic of research in each.

9. Compare cross-sectional and longitudinal studies in terms of the advantages and weaknesses of each.

10. Differentiate among the three types of longitudinal studies by definition and example.

11. Explain how longitudinal studies may be approximated using the cross-sectional design.

12. Depict the research process in a diagram and describe the diagram.

13. Rank order the three basic strategies for gathering data in terms of their frequency in the most recent time period.

14. Identify the basic elements of a research proposal.

SUMMARY

Research design involves developing strategies for executing scientific inquiry. It involves specifying precisely what you want to find out and determining the most efficient and effective strategies for doing so. Appropriate research designs enable the social scientist to make observations and interpret the results.

Social scientists typically have one or more of the following as goals for their research: exploration, description, and explanation. Exploratory studies are often done when a researcher is examining a new interest, or when the subject of study is relatively uncharted. They help to determine the feasibility of a larger scale study and to develop the methods for such a study. The researcher's intent in a descriptive study is to observe and describe some segment of social reality. Explanatory studies are undertaken to identify possible causal variables of a given social phenomenon, thereby contributing to understanding.

Social scientists typically study individual people as their units of analysis, although they do so in aggregate form. But they also frequently study social groups, such as families. Even though the unit of analysis is the group, characteristics of the group may be derived from the characteristics of individual members. Formal social organizations, like a corporation, are also a unit of analysis. Finally, social artifacts are the products of social beings or their behavior and can also be analyzed.

It is critically important to identify the units of analysis in a study accurately. Failure to do so may result in two logical errors: the ecological fallacy and reductionism. Committing the ecological fallacy involves gathering data on one unit of analysis but making assertions regarding another. Reductionism refers to an overly strict limitation on the kinds of concepts and variables to be considered in understanding a social phenomenon. Both errors involve misuse of the unit of analysis.

Regardless of the unit of analysis employed, it is important to specify clearly what is examined. Most social science research concentrates on one of three points of focus: characteristics, orientations, and actions. Characteristics refer to states of being; orientations reflect attitudes and beliefs; and actions reflect actual behaviors.

Another aspect of research design is the time dimension. The major distinction lies between cross-sectional studies (observations at one point in time) and longitudinal studies (observations made at multiple time points). There are three types of longitudinal studies. Trend studies are those that examine changes within some general population over time. Cohort studies examine more specific subpopulations as they change over time. Panel studies examine the same set of people over time. Longitudinal studies are clearly superior for making causal assertions, but approximations to this design are frequently found in cross-sectional studies through such techniques as using simple logic, establishing clarity of time order of the variables, asking retrospective questions, and making age-cohort comparisons.

In short, the research process begins with an interest, idea, or theory, which in turn mandates clear conceptualization and operationalization. Appropriate research designs and sampling strategies must be used. The product is a series of observations, which are processed and analyzed, and the results are linked with the original framework of the study. Potential applications of the results should be considered. Although the research process does not always proceed in such a neat fashion, all these elements must be addressed. In designing a research project, researchers find it useful to assess their own interests, their abilities, and the resources available. Some find that multiple research strategies are the most effective, a process known as triangulation.

Research proposals are used to describe a potential study explicitly. They involve a clear statement of the problem, a literature review, a description of the subjects, a description of the measurement and data collection methods, an outline of the intended analyses, a schedule, and a budget.

TERMS

1. actions
2. characteristics
3. cohort studies
4. cross-sectional studies
5. description
6. ecological fallacy
7. explanation
8. exploration
9. longitudinal studies
10. orientations
11. panel studies
12. reductionism
13. social artifacts
14. trend studies
15. triangulation
16. units of analysis

MATCHING

____ 1. The use of several research methods to test the same findings.

____ 2. The purpose of research that stresses the determination of causes.

____ 3. The "what" or "whom" that is actually studied.

____ 4. An overly strict limitation on the kinds of concepts and variables to be considered in understanding a wide range of human behavior.

____ 5. The attitudes, beliefs, personality traits, prejudices, and predispositions of individuals.

____ 6. Studies in which the units of analysis are studied at one point in time.

____ 7. Longitudinal studies in which independent samples of the same age group are studied at two points in time or more.

____ 8. Longitudinal studies in which the same sample is studied at two points in time or more.

REVIEW QUESTIONS

1. Exploratory studies are done most often for purposes of
   a. predicting future behavior, testing feasibility of a more careful study, developing methods to be used in a more careful study

b. connecting empirical reality with theory, satisfying a researcher's curiosity, developing methods to be used in a more careful study

c. satisfying a researcher's curiosity, testing feasibility of a more careful study, developing methods to be used in a more careful study

d. connecting empirical reality with theory, predicting future behavior, developing methods to be used in a more careful study

e. satisfying a researcher's curiosity, testing feasibility of a more careful study, connecting empirical reality with theory

2. The degree of relationship between two variables is of particular concern in which type of study?
   a. exploratory
   b. descriptive
   c. explanatory
   d. qualitative
   e. panel

3. Researcher Lewis spends three months as a choir member touring Europe to see what off-stage choir member interaction is all about. This is an example of which kind of study?
   a. cohort
   b. cross-sectional
   c. exploratory
   d. descriptive
   e. trend

4. Professor Johannison has just discovered that amount of time spent in social activities has a causal influence on academic performance. This is an example of which kind of study?
   a. explanatory
   b. exploratory
   c. cross-sectional
   d. descriptive
   e. trend

5. If a researcher wanted to find out how much time elderly persons in nursing homes spend interacting with each other, the researcher would conduct which kind of study?
   a. exploratory
   b. cohort

   c.   explanatory
   d.   descriptive
   e.   time-lag

6. Examine each of the following statements and determine the unit of analysis and the point of focus.

Units of analysis:	Points of focus:
a. individual	a. characteristic
b. group	b. orientation
c. organization	c. action
d. artifact	

	UNIT	TOPIC
a. Most Americans believe in God.	____	____
b. Ten percent of the families in a community move within a year.	____	____
c. Church records show that women give more money than do men.	____	____

7. Which of the following *best* reflects the ecological fallacy?
   a.   data gathered from individuals, conclusions drawn about individuals
   b.   data gathered from individuals, conclusions drawn about groups
   c.   data gathered from groups, conclusions drawn about organizations
   d.   data gathered from groups, conclusions drawn about individuals
   e.   data gathered from organizations, conclusions drawn about nations

8. The error of reductionism applies to which one of the following?
   a.   the purpose of research
   b.   qualitative versus quantitative research
   c.   the kinds of concepts or variables examined
   d.   time dimension of research
   e.   topic of research

9. A particular weakness in cross-sectional studies is that
   a.   too often too few people are studied
   b.   too often too few variables are studied
   c.   they are limited to individuals as the units of analysis

d. they are too descriptive and insufficiently explanatory

e. they make it difficult to infer causality

10. Professor Lodwick used the 1990 United States Census and the 1980 Census to compare the average family size. This reflects which type of study?
    a. cross-sectional exploratory
    b. cross-sectional descriptive
    c. trend exploratory
    d. trend descriptive
    e. panel exploratory

11. Which type of study would **best** enable a researcher to assess changes associated with attending college for four years?
    a. cross-sectional
    b. longitudinal
    c. trend
    d. cohort
    e. panel

12. Which one of the following is **not** an appropriate strategy for approximating longitudinal studies when only cross-sectional data are available?
    a. using logical inference
    b. examining the time order of the variables
    c. examining differences in responses of those who return their questionnaires early versus late
    d. examining age differences
    e. asking respondents to recall their pasts

13. Regarding the research cited on type of method used in sociological articles over time, which one of the following is *false*?
    a. surveys have gained in popularity
    b. experimental studies have always been rare
    c. the interpretative method has remained quite constant
    d. the shifts in percentages are substantial in the categories that changed.
    e. all are true

DISCUSSION QUESTIONS

1. Discuss the reasons why a social scientist would do an exploratory study, a descriptive study, and an explanatory study. Select a research topic and show how this topic would be addressed in terms of each of the three purposes of research.

2. Compare the ecological fallacy with reductionism in terms of similarities and differences. Give examples of each. Present a case for one being a more serious error than the other.

3. Professor Nelson is doing a study on the effects of the following variables on the drinking behavior of college students: class level, sex, number of high school extracurricular activities, drug usage in high school, family stability during early adolescence, and religiosity. She has a grant to study 800 college students at one point in time and wishes to make some causal assertions. Discuss how she can approximate a longitudinal study, and discuss the types of causal assertions she can legitimately make. Also discuss the limitations on these assertions. Be specific, and use some or all of the variables in your answer.

4. A fellow student who has not taken research methods comes to you for assistance in developing a research project. Which of the research design issues discussed in this chapter would you suggest he address? Why? In what order? Why? What would be your response to his question: "Which of these is the most important?" Why did you respond as you did?

EXERCISE 4.1

Make up examples for the following combinations of units of analysis and points of focus. Do not use examples from the text or review questions.

UNITS OF ANALYSIS	POINTS OF FOCUS	EXAMPLE
individual	orientation	_____
individual	action	_____
individual	characteristic	_____
group	orientation	_____
group	action	_____
group	characteristic	_____
organization	orientation	_____
organization	action	_____
organization	characteristic	_____
artifact	orientation	_____
artifact	action	_____
artifact	characteristic	_____

EXERCISE 4.2

Select a topic of interest—some characteristic, orientation, or action. Show how this topic would be researched following each of the following designs: cross-sectional, trend, cohort, and panel.

EXERCISE 4.3

Find a research article of interest in one of the social science journals or select one from the reader you are using in this or another social science course. (Your instructor may give you an article or list of articles from which to select.) Make a copy because this article will be used in later exercises; attach the copy to this exercise.

1. Identify the point(s) of focus and explain your answer.

2. Identify the unit(s) of analysis and explain your answer.

3. Identify the independent and dependent variables and explain your answer.

4. Identify which of the following designs were employed and explain your answer: cross-sectional, trend, cohort, panel.

5. Identify which of the three primary methods listed in Table 4-1 in the text (page 106) is evident in the study and explain your answer.

6. Briefly describe any methodological weaknesses apparent at this stage of the course.

EXERCISE 4.4

The data reported below come from the General Social Survey. The question asked was, "Do you think the use of marijuana should be made legal or not?" The question was asked of different random samples in 1976 and 1986.

Should marijuana be legal?	Year 1976	1986
Should	29%	19%
Should not	71%	81%
	100%	100%

1. Summarize the results of the table.

2. Does this table reflect longitudinal or cross-sectional data? If longitudinal, which type? Why?

Chapter 5

Conceptualization and Measurement

OBJECTIVES

1. Restate the argument that anything that exists can be measured.

2. Define measurement and differentiate it from observation.

3. Link the concepts of conception and terms.

4. Differentiate among the following terms: direct observables, indirect observables, constructs, and concepts.

5. Show how indicators and dimensions contribute to the conceptualization process.

6. Outline the logic behind the interchangeability of indicators.

7. Illustrate reification and explain why it is an error.

8. Describe and compare real definitions, nominal definitions, and operational definitions.

9. Select three concepts and develop both nominal and operational definitions for each.

10. Explain why definitions are more problematic for descriptive research than for explanatory research.

11. Differentiate precision from accuracy by definition and example.

12. Define reliability and list four strategies for improving the reliability of measures.

13. Define validity and compare the four types of validity.

SUMMARY

Social scientists believe that anything that exists can be measured. This is accomplished through the twin processes of conceptualization and operationalization. Conceptualization involves specifying what is meant by a concept, while operationalization yields the specific measures. Social scientists also commonly distinguish measurement from observation; the latter is a more global concept, and the former means careful observations for purposes of describing objects and events in terms of the attributes of a variable.

Concept is another term for construct, which is a theoretical creation based on observations and experiences and which generally reflects a shared meaning. Terms are used to enable communication about concepts.

Concepts themselves are not real or measurable; the indicators of a concept provide this function. Indicators are specific measures of the real and observable things that give evidence of the presence or absence of a concept. Seldom can a single indicator capture the full richness of meaning in most concepts. As a result, social scientists develop multiple indicators arranged around logical groupings, which are known as dimensions. Multiple dimensions and multiple indicators contribute to a more sophisticated understanding of our concepts.

To the extent that multiple, interchangeable indicators produce similar findings, researchers can reach the same conclusions about general concepts, even if they disagree about definitions. This stance is based on the assumption that if different indicators all represent the same concept, then all of them will behave the same way that the concept would behave if it were real and observable. Unfortunately, we sometimes fall into the trap that the terms reflecting our concepts have real meanings, an error known as reification.

Three types of definitions contribute to conceptual order. Real definitions reflect the essential nature of a concept but are not very useful in the measurement process. Conceptualization instead depends on nominal and operational definitions. A nominal definition is one that is assigned to a term in a given study, and an operational definition details the specific operations involved in measuring the concept. These elements of conceptualization underscore the process nature of this step and produce conceptual order so that communication and measurement can proceed. Interestingly, definitions are more problematic for descriptive research than for explanatory research.

Social scientists apply several criteria to enhance measurement quality. They strive to develop measures that are both precise and accurate. They pay particular attention to reliability (consistency) and validity (actually measuring the concept of interest). Problems with both appear repeatedly in social research. Reliability can be enhanced by asking people only things they are likely to know, by asking the same information more than once (test-retest method), by randomly assigning items to two sets and comparing the responses in the two sets (split-half method), and by using measures known for their reliability. Consistent application of the research design is also mandatory.

Validity can be enhanced through establishing face validity, whereby measures are compared with common agreements about a concept and with a logical understanding of a concept. Criterion-related validity (or predictive validity) is based on an external criterion. Content validity refers to the extent to which a measure covers the range of meanings included in a concept. Finally, construct validity is based on the way a measure relates to other variables within a system of theoretical relationships.

TERMS

1. accuracy
2. bias
3. concept
4. conception
5. conceptualization
6. constructs
7. construct validity
8. content validity
9. criterion-related validity
10. dimension
11. direct observables
12. face validity
13. indicators
14. indirect observables
15. interchangeability of indicators
16. measurement
17. nominal definition

18. operational definition
19. precision
20. real definition
21. reliability

22. split-half method
23. term
24. test-retest method
25. validity

MATCHING

____ 1. Careful, deliberate observations of the real world for the purpose of describing objects and events in terms of the attributes composing a variable.

____ 2. The process through which we specify what we will mean when we use particular terms.

____ 3. Real, observable things that give evidence of the presence or absence of the concept we are studying.

____ 4. The definition that is assigned a term.

____ 5. The definition that specifies the operations involved in measuring a concept.

____ 6. Reflects the consistency or repeatability of a measure.

____ 7. Reflects the extent to which a measure reflects the concept we wish to measure.

____ 8. What is used to communicate about our conceptions and the things we observe that are related to those conceptions.

REVIEW QUESTIONS

1. Which of the following is *false*?
   a. the concept ethnicity represents the term ethnicity
   b. ethnicity is both a concept and a variable
   c. ethnicity as a variable is composed of attributes
   d. ethnicity may have different definitions
   e. all are true

2. The number of times one swims a week as used to measure physical fitness is an example of a/an
   a. operational definition
   b. indicator
   c. concept
   d. dimension
   e. construct

3. Which of the following is *least* likely to be a dimension of marital happiness?
   a. financial decision making
   b. sexual compatibility
   c. child rearing
   d. couple communication
   e. length of courtship

4. Professor Lewis spends a few weeks working through what she means by feminism. She decides that it includes such areas as equal treatment before the law, equality in the job market, and belief in the equality of men and women. She then develops specific questions for each of these three areas, such that the sum of the items creates a feminism score. In this example, which of the following reflects conceptualization?
   a. the whole process
   b. the term *feminism*
   c. the three basic areas
   d. the calculation of a feminism score
   e. the questions

5. Which of the following *best* reflects interchangeability of indicators?
   a. Joe uses multiple indicators and then deletes two and adds three on the basis of a test for reliability
   b. Cathy decides to use several indicators of one of her variables to improve validity
   c. Lisa decides to use several indicators of both her variables to improve validity
   d. James argues that it really doesn't matter which of the indicators of his dependent variable is used because whatever relationship exists will appear with any of them
   e. Susan argues that indicators can be exchanged across dimensions and that the reliability and validity as well as the basic relationship will not be altered

6. Professor Foxdire has been working with the concept of stress for several years and has seriously worked at developing a precise measure of stress. He then works harder at discovering the real meaning of stress and finally decides that stress is real and his measure genuinely reflects it. What error has he fallen prey to?
   a. mystification of residuals
   b. interchangeability
   c. objectification
   d. ecological fallacy
   e. reification

7. An operational definition includes all *but* which of the following characteristics?
   a. specification of observations
   b. decisions regarding how to observe
   c. colleagues' agreement about what the definition is
   d. decisions regarding interpretation of the observations
   e. logical connection between concept and operational definition

8. Professor Wilson decides to study academic aspiration and, in line with the general thinking on the concept, specifies that she will treat it as the highest degree desired. This is an example of a/an
   a. categorical definition
   b. nominal definition
   c. real definition
   d. empirical definition
   e. operational definition

9. Operational definitions are more problematic for descriptive research than for explanatory research because
   a. interpretations of descriptive statements directly depend on operational definitions used
   b. interpretations of explanatory statements directly depend on the causal connection between concept and operational definition
   c. in explanatory research operationalization of concepts is irrelevant as long as causality is established
   d. descriptive statements demand greater specificity than do explanatory statements
   e. explanatory research deals primarily with relationships between variables and not operational definitions

10. Which one of the following is *false*?
    a. precision is more important in descriptive than in explanatory research
    b. precision is less important than validity
    c. precision parallels validity
    d. operationalization enhances precision
    e. a measure can be precise without being accurate

11. Professor Garcia decides to employ 60 interviewers in his study of teacher militancy. Which one of the following will probably be the *major* measurement concern?
    a. epistemology
    b. validity
    c. reliability
    d. conceptual adequacy
    e. ability to interchange the indicators

12. Personnel Director Putler develops a measure of job satisfaction. She shows it to a couple of other personnel directors to make sure her scale measures what it purports to measure. She is seeking
    a. reliability
    b. precision
    c. face validity
    d. accuracy
    e. indicator correlation

13. Which one of the following statements is *false*? Or are all true?
    a. a measure can be reliable and valid
    b. a measure can be reliable but invalid
    c. a measure can be unreliable and invalid
    d. a measure can be unreliable and valid
    e. all are true

14. Professor Peoples develops a new scale to measure love. When given repeatedly, it generally yields similar results. When correlated with a well-validated love scale, it shows a low correlation. Which one of the following statements is correct?
    a. the scale is reliable but not valid
    b. the scale is valid but not reliable
    c. the scale is both reliable and valid

d.   the scale is neither reliable nor valid

e.   the scale is generalizable but not precise

15. Marketing Analyst Haas tests the validity of her new customer satisfaction
     scale by testing its relationship to other variables found to be related to other
     customer satisfaction scales. She is using which type of validity?

a.   face

b.   criterion-related

c.   content

d.   construct

e.   multidimensional

DISCUSSION QUESTIONS

1. Present a case that we can measure anything that exists. Use examples.

2. Describe what is meant by interchangeability of indicators. Using definitions
    and examples, compare this concept with interchangeability of indexes
    (discussed in Chapter 3).

3. Explain why definitions are more of a problem in descriptive research than in explanatory research.

4. Which is more important, reliability or validity? Why?

EXERCISE 5.1

Select one of the following concepts: religiosity, feminism, patient anxiety, marital happiness. Address each of the following.

1. Describe the conceptualization process you would employ to measure this concept.

2. Provide a nominal definition of the concept.

3. Describe the indicators you would use in developing your operational definition.

EXERCISE 5.2

Quite often a college student's grade point average (GPA) is taken as an indicator of her or his intelligence relative to that of other students. Give some reasons why GPA may **not** be (a) reliable and (b) valid as a measure of the intelligence of college students.

1. Problems of reliability

2. Problems of validity

EXERCISE 5.3

Use the article you used for Exercise 4.3, or find another social science research article (or use the article or list of articles supplied by your instructor). Select one of the concepts in the article and describe the conceptualization and operationalization processes employed. Provide specific examples of dimensions and indicators and of nominal and operational definitions. Assess the reliability and validity of the measure.

EXERCISE 5.4

The concept of attitude toward pornography might be measured with the following four items. Respondents could be asked to indicate if they thought that:

a. sexual materials lead to breakdown of morals
b. sexual materials lead people to commit rape
c. sexual materials provide an outlet for bottled-up impulses
d. sexual materials provide information about sex

1. Speculate about the conceptualization process that produced these items. That is, speculate about the thinking process a social scientist might have gone through to develop these four items to measure attitude toward pornography.

2. Explain how the four types of reliability techniques could be applied to the items.

3. Explain how the four types of validity techniques could be applied to the items.

EXERCISE 5.5

Your task is to count the number of restaurants on some section of a busy commercial street in your area. Your instructor may specify a particular area for you to study.

1. Which street did you choose, or which street did your instructor assign?

2. What are the cross-streets delimiting the section you studied?

3. How many restaurants did you count?

4. Discuss the problem of conceptualization and operationalization in relation to this assignment. How did you define "restaurant" and how did you apply that definition?

Chapter 6

Operationalization

OBJECTIVES

1. Distinguish conceptualization from operationalization.

2. Restate the advice on establishing a range of variation in the operationalization process.

3. List three dimensions for each of two concepts of your choice.

4. Explain why attributes should be exhaustive and mutually exclusive and give examples of each.

5. Differentiate the following four levels of measurement and give an example of each: nominal, ordinal, interval, and ratio.

6. Explain why it is important to know the level of measurement for the variables in a study.

7. Explain when single or multiple indicators should be used to reflect a concept.

8. Differentiate questions from statements by definition and example.

9. Outline the conditions under which open-ended and closed-ended questions are used.

10. List and illustrate several guidelines for asking effective questions.

11. Explain why social desirability is a problem in asking questions.

12. List three guidelines for good questionnaire format.

13. Describe the role of contingency questions and list three principles for their use.

14. Describe the role of matrix questions and list the principles for their use.

15. Explain why the order in which questions are asked is important, and describe how this principle is differentially applied in questionnaires and interviews.

16. List three principles for providing instructions for respondents of surveys.

SUMMARY

The measurement process in social science research includes both conceptualization and operationalization. The former is the refinement and specification of abstract concepts, and the latter is the development of specific research procedures that will result in empirical observations representing those concepts in the real world.

Social scientists have a variety of options available regarding the measurement process. For one, they must decide on the range of variation appropriate for a given concept. This choice is influenced by the nature of the study and the expected distribution of attributes among the subjects under study. Another choice pertains to how fine the distinctions will be among the various possible attributes of a given variable. This choice is also influenced by the purpose of the study, and social scientists err on the side of gathering too much detail rather than too little when they are unsure about how to proceed.

Many times the selection of specific indicators for a variable is quite straightforward because such variables have obvious single indicators. Other variables are better operationalized through composite measures that combine a number of indicators reflecting separate dimensions. In either case, attributes need to be both exhaustive (a complete list of attributes) and mutually exclusive (no overlapping attributes).

Different variables may represent different levels of measurement. Nominal measures employ numbers for classification purposes only; their attributes have only the characteristics of exhaustiveness and mutual exclusiveness. Variables whose attributes may be logically rank-ordered are ordinal measures; the numbers employed reflect relatively more or less of the variable being measured. The actual distance separating attributes in interval measures can be described as being equal, but interval measures have no absolute zero. Ratio measures do have an absolute zero value, enabling the calculation of ratios. It is important to identify the levels of measurement of the variables because analytical techniques vary according to the level of measurement of a variable.

Most concepts are measured through questions and statements. Questions may take one of two forms. Closed-ended questions are easily processed, but sometimes overlook alternative answer categories. Open-ended questions afford a wider range of responses, but they are more difficult to process and may yield irrelevant answers.

Questions should also be relevant to the respondent, very clear, and as short as possible. The respondent should be capable of answering the question, and the researcher should avoid negative items as well as biased items and terms. Combining two questions into one is known as a double-barreled question and produces both confusion for the respondent and ambiguity for the researcher. The researcher should also avoid using questions that promote social desirability--answers that make respondents look good. In the final analysis, the overriding guideline is that questions should reflect the purpose of the study.

Questionnaire format and appearance are critical. Questionnaires that are well organized, uncluttered, and attractive reduce the likelihood that respondents will overlook or ignore items or dispose of the questionnaire. The best format for questions is the use of boxes adequately spaced. Contingency questions can prevent respondents from being confused and annoyed; that is, questions that are relevant to only some of the respondents are identified. A series of questions with the same set of answer categories can be effectively presented through a matrix format, which saves space and time. But occasionally respondents begin marking the same answers without carefully reading the items, a problem known as a response-set.

The order of question presentation is also critical because answers to one question can affect answers to later questions. Also, it is usually best to begin questionnaires with the most interesting set of questions to generate interest, although it is generally best to begin interviews with demographic questions to enhance rapport. Clear instructions at the beginning of a questionnaire, as well as at the beginning of each section, are mandatory. Special situations will require special instructions.

The processes of developing specific measures and refining abstract concepts require a constant exchange across the two levels of abstraction. The end product is a set of measures that is both reliable and valid and that addresses the questions posed in the study.

TERMS

1. biased question
2. closed-ended question
3. composite measure
4. contingency question
5. dimension
6. double-barreled question
7. exhaustive
8. interval measures
9. matrix questions
10. mutually exclusive
11. nominal measures
12. open-ended question
13. operationalization
14. ordinal measures
15. ratio measures
16. social desirability

MATCHING

____ 1. The development of specific research procedures that will result in empirical observations representing concepts in the real world.

____ 2. The quality a variable has when no overlapping attributes exist.

____ 3. Variables whose attributes have only the characteristics of exhaustiveness and mutual exclusiveness.

____ 4. Variables in which the distances separating the attributes are equal.

____ 5. Variables characterized by rank-ordering of attributes.

_____ 6. Measures characterized by the presence of an absolute zero.

_____ 7. The combination of several indicators to represent a concept.

_____ 8. A question that demands a single answer to a combination of questions.

REVIEW QUESTIONS

1. Professor Martin is examining group cohesion. She attempts to refine this concept by giving examples, identifying possible dimensions, and narrowing her focus in terms of the purpose of the study. She is engaging in
   a. measurement
   b. theorizing
   c. conceptualization
   d. operationalization
   e. dimensionalization

2. In operationalizing approval for abortion, Professor Oliver is particularly concerned that the measure will reflect those opposed to abortion as well as those with varying levels of approval. Which operationalization choice is he confronting?
   a. range of variation
   b. number of dimensions
   c. number of indicators
   d. variation between the extremes
   e. interchangeability of indicators

3. "What is your student status?"
   1. Freshman
   2. Sophomore
   3. Junior
   4. Senior
   5. Transfer

   Which of the following **most** accurately describes this question?
   a. it is exhaustive but not mutually exclusive
   b. it is mutually exclusive but not exhaustive
   c. it is both exhaustive and mutually exclusive

d.   it is neither mutually exclusive nor exhaustive
e.   it is both reliable and valid

4. Grade point average reflects which level of measurement?
    a.   nominal
    b.   ordinal
    c.   linear
    d.   ratio
    e.   interval

5. The importance of levels of measurement lies in
    a.   distinguishing qualitative from quantitative research
    b.   clarifying the conceptualization process
    c.   determining which statistical techniques are appropriate
    d.   clarifying the operationalization process
    e.   constructing measures of the same concept at different levels of
         measurement

6. Which one of the following is *false*?
    a.   ordinal measures have the properties of interval measures
    b.   interval measures have the properties of nominal measures
    c.   ratio measures have the properties of ordinal measures
    d.   ordinal measures have the properties of nominal measures
    e.   all are true

7. The *major* problem with closed-ended questions is
    a.   the number of items in the questionnaire
    b.   the number of items per dimension
    c.   the order of the answers
    d.   the structuring of the responses
    e.   response set

8. "How satisfied are you with your working conditions and wages?"
    1.   very satisfied
    2.   somewhat satisfied
    3.   somewhat dissatisfied
    4.   very dissatisfied

    What is the *major* weakness with this item?
    a.   it is double-barreled

b. it is not clear
c. it is too long
d. it is not relevant
e. respondents may not be competent to answer it

9. "How old were you when you first got in a fight with someone other than a sibling?"
   1. 2 or younger
   2. 3-5
   3. 6-7
   4. 8-9
   5. 10 or older
   6. I have never been in a fight

   What is the *major* weakness with this item?
   a. it is double-barreled
   b. it is biased
   c. it is too long
   d. it is not relevant
   e. respondents may not be competent to answer it

10. "The Russians cheated on every agreement to freeze nuclear weapons development since 1930. Don't you agree that the United States should give up on establishing a limitations agreement?"
    1. yes
    2. not sure
    3. no

    What is the *major* weakness with this item?
    a. it is socially desirable
    b. it is too long
    c. it is biased
    d. it is double-barreled
    e. it is not clear

11. "Do you feel that you are basically a kind and loving person?"
    1. all the time
    2. usually
    3. usually not
    4. never

What is the *major* weakness with this item?
a. it is socially desirable
b. it is too long
c. it is not clear
d. it is not mutually exclusive
e. respondents may not be competent to answer it

12. Which one of the following is the *worst* method for providing space for checking responses?
a. boxes
b. parentheses
c. brackets
d. open blanks for check marks
e. all are equally fine

13. Professor Kaled wishes to ask three additional questions of those respondents who have been active in a political organization in the previous year. *Best* to use would be
a. contingency questions
b. matrix questions
c. matched questions
d. separate questionnaires
e. different response sets

14. Response set is *most* likely in which kinds of questions?
a. matrix questions
b. contingency questions
c. closed-ended questions
d. open-ended questions
e. all are susceptible

15. Which one of the following *most* accurately summarizes the role of operationalization in the research process?
a. it occurs before data gathering
b. it occurs as part of theory construction
c. it occurs after hypothesis formulation and through data gathering
d. it occurs as part of conceptualization
e. it occurs throughout the research process

DISCUSSION QUESTIONS

1. Discuss why it is important to consider the levels of measurement of variables in doing research.

2. Discuss the pros and cons of using closed-ended questions and open-ended questions.

3. In this chapter Babbie describes many guidelines for asking questions. Discuss how a researcher could best avoid making the errors he describes. Discuss strategies appropriate before, during, and after the question-writing stage.

EXERCISE 6.1

Select one of the concepts in the General Social Survey (see Appendix 1 in this workbook) that is measured with more than one item. Or select one of the concepts in the article you have used in previous exercises (attach a copy). Assess the adequacy of this measure in terms of the following issues.

1. The range of variation and variation between the extremes.

2. Reliability.

3. Validity.

EXERCISE 6.2

Sue is 20 years old and Mary is 40 years old. Write a simple statement regarding Sue's and Mary's ages that illustrates each of the levels of measurement.

1. Nominal

2. Ordinal

3. Interval

4. Ratio

EXERCISE 6.3

Each of the questionnaire items below has one or more things wrong with it. For each, describe what is wrong. Also, rewrite the item to correct the defects identified.

At the end of the exercise you are asked to identify the appropriate level of measurement for each item.

1. Religion

Protestant	Jewish
Catholic	Episcopalian
Lutheran	Other

Defects:

Rewritten:

2. At what age were you toilet-trained?

   ( ) Before six months old
   ( ) Between six months old and nine months old
   ( ) Between nine months old and one year old
   ( ) Between one year old and one and a half years old
   ( ) Between one and a half years old and two years old
   ( ) Between two years old and three years old
   ( ) Older than three years old
   ( ) Not applicable

Defects:

Rewritten:

3. How much money do you make? $_____

Defects:

Rewritten:

4. Suppose you were in a bookstore and saw a book displayed on a counter near the door that you wanted very much but could not afford. Would you steal it?

( )   Yes   ( ) No

Defects:

Rewritten:

5. Are you a college student or graduate? If so, why did you decide to go to college?

( ) I had a thirst for more knowledge
( ) I wanted to get a better understanding of the world
( ) I was too lazy to get a job

Defects:

Rewritten:

6. Do you agree or disagree that the trouble with welfare is that people get too comfortable and don't want to go back to work, so the government should institute some job-training programs for people on welfare and then set a limited amount of time in which they can learn work skills and get a job?

( ) Agree   ( ) Disagree

Defects:

Rewritten:

7. Do you disagree or agree with the President that the United States shouldn't construct the proposed new anti-ballistic-missile system?

( ) Agree   ( ) Disagree

Defects:

Rewritten:

8. Where do you get most or all of your information about current events in the nation and the world?

( ) Radio   ( ) Newspapers   ( ) Magazines

Defects:

Rewritten:

9. Why do you think big cars are a bad thing for America?

Defects:

Rewritten:

Now go back and determine the appropriate level of measurement for each item. Skip #9 since the level of measurement for that item will be determined by how the answers are eventually coded.

1. _____   5. _____

2. _____   6. _____

3. _____   7. _____

4. _____   8. _____

EXERCISE 6.4

Develop a questionnaire to be given to students on your campus. Write questions on the following concepts:

1. Class level
2. College/division/school (Arts and Science, Business, etc.)
3. Sex
4. Attitudes toward nuclear war (two questions)
5. Attitudes toward various services provided on your campus (e.g., recreational services, health care, etc.) (two or three questions)
6. Number of movies seen
7. Rating of movie enjoyment
8. Problems respondent feels are most serious in America today
9. Attitudes toward one or two political issues that you believe may be relevant to students (two questions)
10. Two questions of your choice

Be sure to include instructions, one contingency question, and some matrix questions. Be sure your questionnaire reflects the advice offered in this chapter.

Chapter 7

Indexes, Scales, and Typologies

OBJECTIVES

1. Link the contents of this chapter with the previous chapters on conceptualization and operationalization (Chapters 5 and 6).

2. List three reasons why composite measures are frequently used in social science research.

3. Differentiate index from scale by definition and example.

4. Describe two misconceptions regarding scaling.

5. List the four steps involved in creating an index.

6. Define and illustrate face validity, unidimensionality, and variance as criteria for selecting items.

7. Describe the rationale and application for employing bivariate relationships among items in index construction.

8. Describe the rationale and application of employing multivariate relationships among items in index construction.

9. Describe how items can be scored in index construction.

10. Describe five strategies for handling missing data in index construction.

11. Compare the rationale and application of item analysis and external validation as strategies for validating an index.

12. Describe the logic and procedures of Likert scaling.

13. Describe the logic and procedures of the semantic differential.

14. Describe the logic and procedures of the Bogardus social distance scale.

15. Describe the logic and procedures of Thurstone scaling.

16. Describe the logic and procedures of Guttman scaling.

17. Explain the coefficient of reproducibility.

18. Explain and illustrate how typologies are used in social science research.

SUMMARY

Composite measures of variables—indexes, scales, and typologies—are created by combining two or more separate empirical indicators into a single measure. Social scientists employ composite measures for several reasons: single indicators are seldom sufficient to measure a complex concept adequately; multiple items extend the range of scores available; and composite measures are efficient strategies for handling multiple items.

Both scales and indexes are typically ordinal composite measures of concepts. Indexes are constructed by accumulating scores assigned to individual attributes, and scales are constructed through the assignment of scores to patterns of attributes. Hence a scale takes advantage of any intensity structure that may exist among the attributes and conveys more information than does an index.

The first step in constructing an index is selecting items. The items must have face validity (logical validity) and be unidimensional (represent only one dimension). Each item should contain some variance, although the amount may be greater for some items than for others. The next step is to examine the relationship among the items to determine if the items are related to each other empirically; this can be done with percentage tables or correlation coefficients. Bivariate analysis of the items is used to identify those items that should be eliminated either because they are unrelated to the other items or because they are so closely related as to be redundant. Multivariate analysis of the items allows the researcher to determine whether each item adds something to the index independently of the other items.

Next comes scoring the items in an index. The researcher must decide on the desirable range of index scores and must attain both a range of measurement in the index as a whole and an adequate number of cases at each point in the index. The researcher must also decide whether to weight the items equally or differentially; equal weighting is typically employed. The scoring process must include provisions for handling missing data. Several strategies are available for doing so, such as excluding those cases with missing data from the construction of the index, treating missing data as one of the available responses, assigning the middle value, or using proportions based on what is observed.

The last step in index construction is to test for validity. In item analysis, the researcher examines the extent to which the composite index is related to the individual items. External validation is employed by testing the index against other indicators of the same concept. External validation sometimes presents a dilemma. If the index is found to be unrelated to the external validator, it may be hard to decide which is invalid—the index or the other indicator.

Likert scaling does not really produce a scale but an index consisting of a series of questionnaire items with a uniformly scored set of ordinal response categories expressing varying degrees of agreement. Composite scores are calculated by adding the individual item scores. One weakness with Likert scaling is that each item is assumed to have the same intensity. Whereas the Likert approach asks respondents to what extent they agree or disagree with a particular statement, the semantic differential asks them to choose between two polar opposites. The researcher using this procedure must determine appropriate dimensions for a concept and should include a set of ordinal response categories representing the range of meaning between the two opposites.

The Bogardus social distance scale is used to measure people's willingness to associate with members of different groups. The scale contains an intensity structure by reflecting varying degrees of closeness tolerated. Hence, one can predict which items were selected on the basis of a single score.

When a logical structure among the indicators is not clear, Thurstone scaling may be employed to develop a format for organizing items that have at least an empirical structure among them. Experts are asked to assign numerical scores to many indicators of the same variable; this score reflects how strongly the item reflects the concept. Items on which there is little agreement are eliminated as ambiguous, and several of the remaining items are selected to represent each scale score from the lowest value to the highest value. Scores are generally assigned on the basis of the items selected that have the highest value. Thurstone scaling is infrequently used today because of the time required to construct the scale.

Guttman scaling is also based on the fact that some items may prove to be "harder" indicators of a concept than others. An important objective of Guttman scaling is to maximize the reproducibility of response patterns from a single scale score. The coefficient of reproducibility reflects the percentage of original responses that could be reproduced by knowing the scale scores used to summarize them. Coefficients above .90 are necessary to conclude that a scale exists.

Whereas indexes and scales provide measures of a single dimension, typologies are often employed to examine the intersection of two or more dimensions. Typologies are very useful analytical tools and can be easily used as independent variables, although the fact that they are not unidimensional makes it difficult to analyze them as dependent variables.

TERMS

1. Bogardus social distance scale
2. coefficient of reproducibility
3. composite measure
4. data reduction devices
5. external validity
6. face validity
7. Guttman scaling
8. index
9. index validity
10. intensity structure
11. item analysis
12. Likert scale
13. mixed types
14. scale
15. scale types
16. semantic differential
17. Thurstone scaling
18. typology
19. unidimensionality
20. variance

MATCHING

___ 1. The general class of ordinal measures constructed through the simple accumulation of scores assigned to individual attributes.

___ 2. The general class of measures constructed through the assignment of scores to patterns of attributes; hence it contains an intensity structure.

___ 3. The criterion for choosing indicators that emphasizes the importance of selecting items that logically reflect the concept being measured.

___ 4. The element of a composite measure that indicates that the measure reflects only one dimension.

___ 5. A measure of internal validity that involves examining the extent to which the composite measure is related to (or predicts responses to) the items in the index itself.

___ 6. The generalizability of the results of a measure.

___ 7. A type of index in which response categories reflect intensity of agreement and that assumes that each item has the same intensity as the others.

___ 8. A measure summarizing the intersection of two or more dimensions.

REVIEW QUESTIONS

1. The *major* reason for using composite measures is
   a. they enhance reliability
   b. they enhance external validity
   c. they yield validity coefficients
   d. they yield more comprehensive measures with a wider range of scores
   e. they enhance the conceptualization process, thereby strengthening the theory

2. Which of the following is *not* a composite measure?
   a. scales
   b. indicators

c. indexes
d. typologies
e. all are composite measures

3. The key difference between scales and indexes is that scales
   a. are generally longer
   b. require more conceptualization
   c. take into account the different strengths of the indicators
   d. are more valid and reliable
   e. assist in building typologies

4. Professor Leitner has developed several items to measure self-concept and checks with a few experts to make sure that his items logically represent self-concept. Which criterion of item selection is he using?
   a. unidimensionality
   b. face validity
   c. internal strength
   d. reproducibility
   e. variance

5. In performing bivariate analyses of items, which is the *most* desirable outcome?
   a. some relationships should be low, but most should be moderate
   b. none should be negligibly correlated, but most should be moderately correlated
   c. all should be very strongly related
   d. all but a few should be very strongly correlated
   e. all should be strongly correlated

6. Which of the following should occur after examining the bivariate relationships among items but before combining items into an index?
   a. calculating a coefficient of reproducibility
   b. validating the index
   c. examining multivariate relationships among items
   d. assessing the reliability of the items
   e. examining response patterns across the answer categories per item

7. The two basic decisions to be made in index scoring are
   a. range of scores and weighting of items
   b. weighting of items and number of items

c. number of items and scalability
d. scalability and validity
e. validity and range of scores

8. Professor Bigelow examines the extent to which each item in her fatalism index correlates with the index. Which strategy for index validation is she using?
   a. split-half
   b. parallel forms
   c. item analysis
   d. external validation
   e. face validation

9. Professor Strike wishes to develop a composite measure of adjustment to retirement such that an ordinal scale can be calculated based on items with the same or similar ranges of intensity. Which of the following would be *best*?
   a. semantic differential
   b. Guttman scale
   c. Bogardus social distance scale
   d. Thurstone scale
   e. Likert scale

10. Professor Howery wishes to develop a composite measure of teaching effectiveness by using several dimensions, each with several possible answers between two extremes. The polar extremes are to be labeled. Which of the following would be *best*?
    a. semantic differential
    b. Guttman scale
    c. Bogardus social distance scale
    d. Thurstone scale
    e. Likert scale

11. Professor Delaney wishes to construct a composite measure of job satisfaction but is particularly concerned that the items selected reflect equal intervals. He does this by having experts rate each of the items and then he selects 11 items to represent the range of scores. Which of the following did he use?
    a. semantic differential
    b. Guttman scale
    c. Bogardus social distance scale

d. Thurstone scale
e. Likert scale

12. Professor Feyen wishes to develop a composite measure of abortion support such that she can accurately predict which items a respondent agrees with based on the score. Which of the following would be *best*?
    a. semantic differential
    b. Guttman scale
    c. Bogardus social distance scale
    d. Thurstone scale
    e. Likert scale

13. The key difference between typologies and composite measures is that typologies
    a. are more valid
    b. are more reliable
    c. reflect interval and ratio levels of measurement and hence allow more powerful statistics
    d. contribute more to conceptual clarification
    e. are built with more than one variable

14. One particular weakness of typologies is that
    a. they have little validity
    b. they have little reliability
    c. it is difficult to use them as dependent variables
    d. it is difficult to use them as independent variables
    e. they are difficult to analyze empirically

DISCUSSION QUESTIONS

1. Give three reasons for the frequent use of indexes and scales in social science research.

2. What do indexes and scales have in common? How are they different?

3. Describe the four steps in constructing an index: (1) selecting possible items, (2) examining their empirical relationships, (3) combining some items into an index, and (4) validating the index. Provide specific advice for completing each step.

4. Compare and contrast the following scaling procedures: Likert, Thurstone, and Guttman. For each, note purpose, advantages, disadvantages, and procedures.

5. Describe the utility of typologies.

EXERCISE 7.1

The chapter reviews four basic steps in constructing an index: (1) selecting possible items, (2) examining their empirical relationships, (3) combining some items into an index, and (4) validating the index. You are to apply these steps to the three items in the General Social Survey codebook (see Appendix 1 of this workbook) that measure attitudes toward pornography. The items are "PORNINF," "PORNRAPE," and "PORNOUT." Your instructor will advise you to complete all or only some of these steps.

1. Regarding item selection, assess these items in terms of face validity, unidimensionality, and variance. To assess variance, you will have to run a FREQUENCIES procedure on the items (see Exercise 15.3 in this guide and Appendix H in the text).

2. Regarding the bivariate relationships among the items, assess these relationships with the CROSSTABS procedure (see Exercise 15.4 in this guide and Appendix H in the text). Present the tables below and interpret the results.

3. Regarding the multivariate (in this case trivariate) relationships among the items, use "PORNINF" as the criterion variable (like Babbie used "basic mechanics" in Figure 7-4). The following SPSS^x program will produce the results:

CROSSTABS   TABLES=PORNINF BY PORNRAPE BY PORNOUT
OPTIONS 3 4

For the sake of simplicity, the results should be presented in the following form, although other forms would also be appropriate. Remember that column percentages will not necessarily total 100% since the numbers in your table will only represent the percent who say "Yes" to the "PORNINF" item.

% "Yes" on PORNINF

		PORNRAPE	
		Yes	No
PORNOUT	Yes	___	___
	No	___	___

Interpret the results:

4. Regarding index scoring, apply the discussion in the text to this example. Be specific on how the index will be scored. Use the COMPUTE card to score the index. You may wish to RECODE the variables first so that "No"=0 and "Yes"=1 (see Appendix H in the text for details). Present a frequency distribution of your index and interpret the results. **Note**: in your RECODE statement, be sure to recode 0 to 9 so that 9 will be the new missing value for these variables (0 is the original missing value code). Then follow the RECODE statement with a MISSING VALUES statement noting the 9 as the new missing value for these variables.

5. Regarding index validation via item analysis, validate one of the items by using the index as the independent variable and the selected item as the dependent variable. Use the CROSSTABS procedure. Present and analyze the results.

6. Regarding index validation via external validation, validate the index with either political conservatism ("POLVIEWS") or with having seen an X-rated movie ("XMOVIE"). If you use "POLVIEWS," recode attributes 1, 2, and 3 to 1 (liberal); 4 to 2 (moderate); and 5, 6, and 7 to 3 (conservative). Present and analyze the results.

EXERCISE 7.2

Your assignment is to use the RELIABILITY procedure in SPSS[x] (see Appendix H in the text) to test the internal consistency among the four satisfaction items in the General Social Survey (see Appendix 1). Be sure to define value 8 as missing. Your program should resemble the following:

```
RELIABILITY   VARIABLES=SATFAM SATFRND SATJOB SATFIN/
   SCALE(SATIS)=SATFAM SATFRND SATJOB SATFIN/
STATISTICS 1 4 5 8 9
```

1. As noted in the text and in Appendix H in the text, a reliable index has at least three characteristics. First, each item is positively correlated with every other item. Second, each item is positively correlated with the overall scale score. Third, all possible split-half index scores of these items are well correlated. Analyze your results for the satisfaction items in terms of these three characteristics.

2. Use the COMPUTE procedure to create a satisfaction scale. Then run a FREQUENCIES procedure on this scale and present and analyze the results.

EXERCISE 7.3

You are to develop a semantic differential scale for a concept of interest. Be sure to follow the advice presented in the chapter.

1. List at least five dimensions that adequately reflect your concept.

2. Set up the items to resemble Figure 7-5, and include both the polar opposite terms and the ratings in between.

3. Describe how you would score the results.

EXERCISE 7.4

Develop a typology in an area of interest. Explain why you selected the two or more dimensions in your typology. Present your typology in a format like that in Table 7-4. Explain the typology and how it could be used in a research study. Be specific.

Chapter 8

The Logic of Sampling

OBJECTIVES

1. Document the historical connection between sampling and political polling.

2. Describe the logic of probability sampling, and include heterogeneity and representativeness in your response.

3. List two advantages of probability sampling over nonprobability sampling.

4. Define an EPSEM sample.

5. Define each of the following terms and explain its role in probability sampling: element, population, study population, sampling unit, sampling frame, observation unit, and variable.

6. Differentiate a parameter from a statistic.

7. Define sampling error and show how confidence levels and confidence intervals are used in interpreting sampling errors.

8. Using probability sampling theory, describe the sampling distribution.

9. Define and illustrate the binomial sampling distribution.

10. Explain how to interpret a standard error in terms of the normal distribution.

11. Present an argument that the survey uses of probability theory are not entirely justified technically.

12. Restate the cautions regarding making generalizations from sampling frames to populations.

13. Describe simple random sampling and list two reasons why it is seldom used.

14. Summarize the steps in using a table of random numbers.

15. Describe systematic sampling, and employ the concepts of sampling interval, sampling ratio, and periodicity in your description.

16. Link stratified sampling with the principle of heterogeneity and describe how this strategy is executed.

17. Identify the major advantage of multistage cluster sampling and describe how this procedure is executed.

18. Present guidelines for balancing the number of clusters and the cluster size in multistage cluster sampling.

19. Explain why a researcher might use probability proportionate to size sampling, and explain the logic behind this strategy.

20. Outline the rationale for disproportionate sampling and weighting, and note the dangers in using these strategies.

21. List the basic methods for weighting.

22. Describe and illustrate each of the following types of nonprobability sampling: purposive (judgmental) sampling, quota sampling, and available subjects sampling.

SUMMARY

Having specified what is to be studied, the next task in the research process is selecting a sample. Sampling affords the social scientist the capability of describing a larger population based on only a selected portion of that population. Two broad types of sampling methods are probability sampling and nonprobability sampling. Some sampling methods are more accurate than others; the early failures and the more recent successes of political pollsters illustrate the refinement of sampling procedures and the increasing reliance on probability methods.

Probability sampling occurs when every element has an equal and known chance of being selected (an EPSEM sample). It is grounded in the heterogeneity found in the units of analysis social scientists examine. Probability sampling reduces biases, enhances the representativeness of a sample, and permits a statistical estimate of the accuracy or representativeness of a sample.

Probability sampling requires familiarity with several components. An element is that unit about which information is collected, and it is typically the unit of analysis of the study. In contrast, an observation unit is an element or aggregation of elements from which information is collected; the observation unit and the element are often the same.

There are two levels to which a sample can be generalized. A study population is the aggregation of elements from which the sample is actually collected. A population is a theoretically specified aggregation of study elements. A sampling frame is the actual listing of sampling units from which the sample is collected and usually corresponds to the study population, although many sampling frames fail to include all the elements in a study population.

Multistage sampling requires multiple sampling units, those elements considered for selection at some stage of the sampling process. The summary description of a given variable for a given population is known as a parameter, and the analogous description for a sample is known as a statistic.

The calculation and interpretation of sampling error lies at the root of probability sampling theory and is grounded in the principle of the sampling distribution. The sampling distribution dictates that sample statistics will be normally distributed around the population mean. Probability theory also provides formulas for estimating how closely the sample statistics are clustered around the true population value. This is accomplished through the use of confidence levels (how confident we are that our sample estimate is within a set number of standard errors of the population value) and confidence intervals (the range between the upper and lower values for a given level of confidence).

However, probability theory operates on a number of assumptions that are seldom met in real-life survey situations. For example, an infinitely large population, an infinite number of samples, and sampling with replacement are assumed. Probability theory is useful only to the extent that the researcher can actually select a probability sample. Difficulties in securing an adequate sampling frame put constraints on this requirement. Inadequacies such as omissions or duplications of elements have a crucial bearing on whether the sample findings can be generalized to the population.

Simple random sampling is generally assumed in probability applications. This strategy involves assigning a number to each element and using a table of random numbers to select elements for the sample. But simple random sampling is seldom used because it is not generally feasible and it may not be the most accurate method. Systematic sampling is generally preferred over simple random sampling because of simplicity. Once the sampling ratio (the proportion of the population) is determined, the researcher simply selects the elements corresponding to the sampling interval (the distance between elements selected), with the first element selected with a table of random numbers. But researchers must be on guard for periodicity, a cyclical pattern that coincides with the sampling interval.

Stratification may be used with both these strategies, and it increases representativeness by first organizing the sampling frame into homogeneous groups reflecting variables that may be related to the variables under study. Such homogeneous groupings reduce sampling error.

Multistage cluster sampling is most useful when no master list exists to provide a sampling frame. The researcher employs multiple sampling units such that groups of elements are sampled at different stages; the element is the final stage. But this design produces higher sampling errors because each stage yields additional sampling error. A general guideline is to maximize the number of clusters selected while decreasing the number of elements selected per cluster, because clusters tend to be homogeneous. Cluster designs may employ either simple random or systematic sampling, with or without stratification at any of the stages.

When clusters are of varying sizes, it is important to vary the procedure by employing probability proportionate to size sampling. In this modification, larger clusters are given a greater chance of being selected, but the same number of elements are still selected from each cluster. Sometimes a researcher may deliberately or inadvertently overrepresent a segment of the population. When this occurs, differential weighting can be used to correct for the disproportionate sampling.

Many research situations preclude the use of probability sampling, especially when it is impossible to create sampling frames. In such situations, researchers employ nonprobability sampling strategies. Purposive (or judgmental) sampling occurs when a researcher selects a sample based on his or her own knowledge of the population, its elements, or the nature of the research study. Quota sampling strives to attain representativeness by constructing a matrix representing one or more characteristics of the target population, and then collecting data from persons having the required characteristics of a given cell. Researchers also sometimes rely on available subjects. Though frequently called "random," a better term would be "haphazard."

TERMS

1. available subjects sampling
2. binomial sampling distribution
3. confidence interval
4. confidence level
5. disproportionate sampling
6. element
7. EPSEM sample
8. heterogeneity
9. homogeneity
10. multistage cluster sampling
11. nonprobability sampling
12. observation unit
13. parameter
14. periodicity
15. population
16. probability proportionate to size sampling
17. probability sampling
18. purposive sample
19. quota sampling
20. random selection
21. representativeness
22. sampling
23. sampling bias
24. sampling distribution
25. sampling error
26. sampling frame
27. sampling interval
28. sampling ratio
29. sampling unit
30. simple random sampling
31. standard error
32. statistic
33. stratified sampling
34. stratum
35. study population
36. systematic sampling
37. variable
38. weighting

MATCHING

____ 1. Another term for probability samples that employ the equal probability of selection method.

____ 2. The theoretically specified aggregation of survey elements to which results obtained from the sample are generalized.

____ 3. The element or aggregation of elements from which information is collected.

____ 4. The summary description of a given variable in a survey sample.

____ 5. The sampling method that employs the EPSEM principle.

____ 6. A probability method of sampling in which every *k*th element in the total list is chosen for the sample.

____ 7. A probability method of sampling in which the researcher ensures that appropriate numbers of elements are drawn from homogeneous subsets of the population.

____ 8. Stopping people at a street corner is an example of this type of probability sampling.

REVIEW QUESTIONS

1. The purpose of sampling is to
   a. enhance reliability of measurements
   b. enhance validity of measurements
   c. select a set of people with a range of characteristics
   d. select a set of people who have the same characteristics as the group they are taken from
   e. extend the quality of conceptualization and measurement

2. The failure of several political polls to predict election victories accurately prior to 1950 was due *primarily* to
   a. too small samples
   b. failure to use probability designs

c. use of wrong nonprobability designs
d. poor timing
e. faulty questionnaire construction

3. The *key* feature of probability sampling is that
   a. large samples are taken
   b. a large proportion of the larger population is selected
   c. everyone has an equal chance of being selected
   d. sampling error is eliminated
   e. people are chosen systematically

4. Professor Rosenberg takes a random sample of students from five Michigan public universities and colleges. He then phrases his report in terms of "all Michigan college students." To what group of elements is he generalizing?
   a. parameter
   b. population
   c. study population
   d. sampling unit
   e. sampling frame

5. Professor Dorfman did a study on class level and dating at Alexander University. He used the student directory and selected every 15th student. He then mailed questionnaires to them with two follow-ups. He contacted the registrar's office to find out how many students were not listed in the directory. Which one of the following is the sampling frame?
   a. the students on the registrar's list
   b. students both in the directory and not in the directory
   c. the student directory
   d. Alexander University
   e. sampling

6. Inadequate sampling frames yield problems in establishing
   a. generalizability
   b. theoretical relevance
   c. accurate hypotheses
   d. adequate measurements
   e. all of the above

7. The principle of sampling distribution suggests that
   a. one sample is as good as another

b.   many samples of the same population will yield less error
c.   many samples of the same population will yield values evenly spread out across the confidence interval
d.   many samples of the same population will yield statistics that will fall around the population value in a known way
e.   many samples of the same population will yield a lower sampling error than just one sample

8. Which one of the following distributions of whites and nonwhites in a sample would reflect the most sampling error?
    a.   90-10
    b.   80-20
    c.   70-30
    d.   60-40
    e.   50-50

9. Professor Gherkey calculated a sampling error of 2 in her study on the proportion of students who voted in the last election. She found that 45 percent voted. What is the 95 percent confidence interval?
    a.   41-49
    b.   43-47
    c.   39-51
    d.   44-46
    e.   42-48

10. Professor Andrea did a study on the religious behaviors in one Reformed church. She numbered the members and programmed the computer to generate a set of random numbers and print out address labels. Which type of sampling did she use?
    a.   simple random
    b.   systematic
    c.   stratified
    d.   cluster
    e.   purposive

11. Professor Connally plans to select a systematic sample of 500 students from a list of 2,000. The sampling ratio would be
    a.   4
    b.   10
    c.   8

d. one-fourth

e. none of the above

12. Professor Simpson wishes to take a sample of university students at one university. His main objective is to make sure that the sample is very representative of the larger population in terms of class level and GPA. Which sampling design would be best?
   a. simple random
   b. systematic
   c. stratified
   d. cluster
   e. snowball

13. Consideration of sampling units is particularly relevant for which type of sampling?
   a. cluster
   b. systematic
   c. stratified
   d. proportional
   e. simple random

14. Professor Gorenpinsky is interested in doing a study comparing male and female members of the National Organization For Women. Because few men belong, he takes three-fourths of the men but only one-thirtieth of the women, selecting each segment randomly. Which one of the following *best* describes the principle he used?
   a. stratification
   b. systematic sampling
   c. grouping
   d. clustering
   e. weighting

15. Professor Mallory determines the distribution of students on five variables. She then selects students who fill the pre-established proportions of people in each combination of variables. Which strategy did she use?
   a. haphazard
   b. purposive
   c. stratified
   d. quota
   e. weighting

DISCUSSION QUESTIONS

1. Suppose you were asked by the principal of a local high school to do a survey of the student body. The principal believes it is sufficient to stop students on their way to the library and hand out the questionnaire. You argue for a probability sample instead. State your argument, and give at least two reasons why probability sampling might be preferred. Be sure your analysis incorporates the text discussion on the logic of probability sampling.

2. Discuss the differences between a population, a study population, and a sampling frame. Use examples. Also discuss the cautions that should be applied in generalizing from the sampling frame to the study population and the population.

3. Explain what a sampling distribution is. Why is it an important concept in making inferences from a sample to a population? Link your analysis to the text discussion on probability sampling theory.

4. Determine which of the nonprobability sampling designs is the most representative and explain why.

EXERCISES 8.1 and 8.2

The list of faculty below (taken from the 1988 *Guide to Graduate Departments of Sociology*) is to be used in Exercises 8.1 and 8.2.

1. Andrew Abbott
2. Walter Abbott
3. E.W. Abdul-Mu'min
4. Theodore Abel
5. Nicholas Abercrombie
6. Philip Ablett
7. Mitchel Abolafia
8. Mark Abrahamson
9. Elliot Abrams
10. Harold Abramson
11. Baha Abu-Laban
12. Sharon Abu-Laban
13. Janet Abu-Lughod
14. Joseph Aceves
15. Joan Acker
16. Robert Ackerman
17. Alan Acock
18. Gene Acuff
19. Barry Adam
20. Heribert Adam
21. Donald Adamchak
22. Raymond Adamek
23. Bert Adams
24. E. Merie Adams
25. Rebecca Adams
26. Kiku Adatto
27. David Aday
28. Ronald Aday
29. Daniel Adelson
30. Judith Adler
31. Patricia Adler
32. Peter Adler
33. Madeline Adriance
34. Marilyn Affleck
35. Ben Agger
36. Robert Agnew
37. Adalberto Aguirre
38. Benigno Aguirre
39. Bashiruddin Ahmed
40. Jim Aho
41. Constance Ahrons
42. Angela Aidala
43. Stephen Aigner
44. Michael Aiken
45. Lilialyce Akers
46. Ronald Akers
47. Richard Alba
48. Daniel Albas
49. Don Albrecht
50. Sandra Albrecht
51. Stan Albrecht
52. Joan Aldous
53. Bruce Aldrich
54. Howard Aldrich
55. Delores Aldridge
56. Manuel Alers-Montalvo
57. Nicholas Alex
58. C. Norman Alexander
59. Francesca Alexander
60. Jeffrey Alexander
61. Karl Alexander
62. M. Jacqueline Alexander
63. Robert R. Alford
64. Robert W. Alford
65. Badr-El-Din Ali
66. Ernest Alix
67. Anton Allahar
68. Janicemarie Allard
69. Robert Allegrucci
70. Donald F. Allen
71. Donald S. Allen
72. Francis Allen

EXERCISE 8.1

Review the box in the text on using a table of random numbers (pages 212-213). Using the list of faculty names above and a table of random numbers (see Appendix D in the text), select a simple random sample of ten names.

As you select your sample, you will move through the list of random numbers in the random numbers table. Record below **all** the numbers that you used from the table before you had the numbers necessary for your sample. Place an asterisk beside the numbers from this original list that you actually used in selecting the names for your sample.

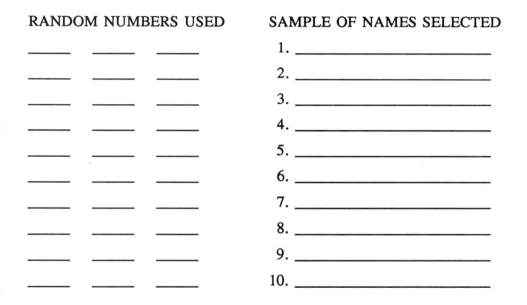

RANDOM NUMBERS USED

SAMPLE OF NAMES SELECTED

1. _____

2. _____

3. _____

4. _____

5. _____

6. _____

7. _____

8. _____

9. _____

10. _____

Briefly explain the procedure you followed to obtain the above sample of names.

EXERCISE 8.2

Using the list of faculty names, select a stratified systematic sample of approximately ten names, beginning with a random start. The stratification variable, in this case, is sex.

First reorganize the list of names by sex. This can most easily be done by simply reorganizing the numbers of the names.

Reorganized list:

Please fill in the requested information.

1. The sampling interval: _____

2. The random start: _____

3. The list of names selected:

    1. _____

    2. _____

    3. _____

    4. _____

5. _____

6. _____

7. _____

8. _____

9. _____

10. _____

NOTE: Correctly drawn systematic samples in this case might result in the selection of 10 or 11 names.

Briefly explain the procedure you used in obtaining the above sample.

EXERCISE 8.3

You have received a grant to study drug usage among college students in America. Describe the tratified cluster sample you would use. Stratify on at least two variables. Sample at least two stages, including the final sampling unit. Describe why you made the decisions you did. Discuss the limitations of your sample.

EXERCISE 8.4

Locate the social science research article that you have used in previous exercises and attach a copy to this exercise. Apply the following sampling issues and concepts to your article. Warning: Not all social science research articles are appropriate for this assignment since many do not completely describe sampling procedures.

1. Describe briefly the population and study population that the study analyzed.

2. Describe the sampling frame used in the selection of the sample. Does this differ from the population as described in #1? How?

3. Describe the type of sampling design used and explain why it was used. Also discuss any particular advantages and/or disadvantages this design yielded.

4. Briefly interpret and assess the standard errors reported, if any.

5. Determine the extent to which the generalizations made are appropriate for the sampling frame used.

Part 3

Modes of Observation

Chapter 9

Experiments

OBJECTIVES

1. Give several examples showing that the experimental mode of observation is particularly appropriate for explanatory purposes.

2. Describe and illustrate with an example the three major pairs of components in the classical experiment.

3. Give an example of the double-blind experiment and indicate why such a design would be used.

4. Contrast the following three strategies for selecting subjects: probability sampling, randomization, and matching.

5. Note the feature that the preexperimental designs have in common, and define and develop examples of each of the following three designs: one-shot case study, one-group pretest-posttest design, and static group comparison.

6. Explain how the following factors may threaten internal validity: history, maturation, testing, instrumentation, statistical regression, selection biases, experimental mortality, causal time-order, diffusion or imitation of treatments, compensation, compensatory rivalry, and demoralization.

7. Show how the classical experiment handles each of these problems of internal invalidity.

8. Compare the following true experimental designs: classical design, Solomon four-group design, and posttest-only control group design.

9. Show how the true experimental designs address the problem of external validity.

10. List three modifications possible to the basic experimental design.

11. Explain how and why focus groups are used.

12. Describe how natural experiments occur and give two examples.

13. Examine the strengths and weaknesses of the experimental method.

SUMMARY

Experimentation involves taking action and observing the consequences of that action. Experiments are particularly well suited to research topics with limited and clearly defined concepts and hypotheses. The experimental model closely parallels the traditional view of science and is particularly appropriate for explanatory research.

The classical experiment involves three major pairs of elements. Such a design examines the effect of an independent variable (the experimental stimulus) on a dependent variable. Both must be clearly defined. Experimental subjects are randomly assigned to an experimental group and a control group, and both are pretested and posttested on the dependent variable. Control groups are used to control for the effects of the experiment itself. One effect that the experimental stimulus may have is known as the Hawthorne effect, in which attention to subjects of any type may affect posttest scores. Double-blind experimental designs are also used to control the effect of the design. In this design neither the subjects nor the experimenters know which is the experimental group and which is the control group.

The cardinal rule for selecting subjects is to maximize the comparability of the experimental and control groups. This can be achieved through three strategies. Probability sampling involves random selection of subjects for the two groups from a sampling frame; it is seldom used. However recruited, subjects may be randomly assigned to either the experimental group or the control group, a technique known as randomization. Third, subjects in the two groups may be matched on variables thought to influence the dependent variable, which is accomplished through the use of a quota matrix. Randomization is the preferred strategy.

Many social scientific experiments employ what are known as preexperimental designs, so called because they lack a legitimate control group and random assignment. The one-shot case study includes a single group of subjects measured on a dependent variable following the occurrence of some experimental stimulus. The one-group pretest-posttest design adds a pretest for the experimental group but still lacks a control group. The static-group comparison includes a "control group," but neither group is pretested, and subjects are not randomly assigned to each.

Preexperimental designs are particularly prone to internal invalidity. A variety of factors produce such invalidity. Historical events may occur during the course of the experiment that may confound the experimental results. Maturation may also occur, whereby subjects become more tired, bored, or changed in some other respect. Often the process of testing and retesting will itself influence people's behavior. Or the measures themselves may not be reliable and valid, a problem known as instrumentation.

Statistical regression becomes a problem when subjects are selected for their extreme scores on the dependent variable. Selection biases enter with many of the methods for selecting subjects. Sometimes subjects drop out of an experiment, known as experimental mortality. Occasionally the causal time order is not entirely clear, and sometimes diffusion occurs when subjects in the two groups communicate with each other. Experimenters sometimes decide to compensate the control group, and sometimes subjects in the control group deprived of the experimental stimulus may try to compensate for a missing stimulus by working harder (known as compensatory rivalry). Finally, demoralization may set in as feelings of deprivation among the control group result in their giving up.

The classical design involves an experimental group and a control group, both randomly assigned and pretested, and effectively manages the sources of internal invalidity noted above. Two other true experimental designs are the Solomon four-group design and the posttest-only control group design. The former effectively manages the interaction between the testing and the experimental stimulus by adding two additional groups, neither pretested but both posttested and one receiving the experimental stimulus. The posttest-only control group design involves assigning subjects randomly to an experimental and a control group but pretesting neither. These two designs are better than the others in terms of external validity, also known as generalizability.

Social scientists sometimes employ focus groups to participate in a guided discussion of a topic. These groups typically involve about a dozen participants to help the researcher better understand an issue. As such, they provide a more natural and less structured approach for eliciting people's reactions.

In their pure form, experiments are usually conducted in a laboratory setting with a high level of researcher control. But not all social phenomena are subject to this kind of control. As a result, researchers sometimes rely on natural experiments to study effects of events that occur in the real world.

The major advantage of experiments is the clear isolation of the experimental variable and its impact on the dependent variable. Experiments are also easily duplicated, which enhances reliability and validity. The greatest weakness of experiments lies in their artificiality. It is not always clear how well the results of laboratory experiments can be generalized to settings outside the laboratory.

TERMS

1. compensatory rivalry
2. control group
3. dependent variable
4. diffusion
5. double-blind experiment
6. experimental group
7. experimental model
8. experimental mortality
9. experimental stimulus
10. external validity
11. focus groups
12. Hawthorne effect
13. history
14. independent variable
15. instrumentation
16. internal invalidity
17. matching
18. maturation
19. natural experiment
20. one-group pretest-posttest design
21. one-shot case study
22. placebo
23. posttesting
24. posttest-only control group design
25. preexperimental designs
26. pretesting
27. quota matrix
28. randomization
29. selection biases
30. Solomon four-group design
31. static-group comparison
32. statistical regression
33. testing

MATCHING

___ 1. In an experiment, the group that receives the experimental stimulus.

___ 2. In an experiment, the group that does not receive the experimental stimulus.

___ 3. The method used to ensure comparability of the experimental and control groups; it assumes that every subject has an equal and known chance of being assigned to either group.

___ 4. A group of designs that deviate from the principles of the classical design.

___ 5. A type of experiment in which neither the experimenter nor the subjects know who receives the experimental stimulus.

___ 6. That which reflects the possibility that the conclusions drawn from the experimental results may not accurately reflect what has gone on in the experiment itself.

___ 7. A bias in which there is a loss of subjects in an experiment.

___ 8. A bias in which subjects in the experimental group may pass on some of the experimental stimulus to members of the control group.

REVIEW QUESTIONS

1. Which one of the following is *false* regarding experimentation?
   a. the experimental model is closely related to the traditional image of science
   b. experimentation is especially appropriate for hypothesis testing
   c. it is better suited for explanatory than descriptive research
   d. it is especially notable for high researcher control
   e. all are true

2. Which one of the following is *not* an aspect of the classical experimental design?
   a. independent and dependent variables

b. experimental and control groups
c. high internal validity and high external validity
d. pretesting and posttesting
e. all are true

3. Professor Stauffer performed an experiment on learning by varying the mode of instruction. She did this for three different grade levels. Which of the following is the experimental stimulus?
   a. mode of instruction
   b. amount learned
   c. anxiety level
   d. grade level
   e. control variable

4. The importance of having a pretest to compare with posttest results lies in
   a. making the sample more random
   b. comparing the results across pretests
   c. comparing pretest results with posttest results across groups in the experiment
   d. making the two groups more equal
   e. comparing the pretest with pretests in other experiments to establish generalizability

5. An experimenter wanted to see the effects of caffeine intake on the arousal state of her subjects. She randomly assigned subjects to the experimental and control groups and administered caffeine-rich soda to one group of subjects and caffeine-free soda to the other group; she then compared the arousal states of the members of both groups. This is an example of a
   a. posttest-only control group
   b. pretest-posttest design
   c. double-blind experiment
   d. classical design
   e. static-group comparison

6. In the above experiment, caffeine-rich soda and caffeine-free soda, respectively, are the
   a. independent variable and dependent variable
   b. experimental stimulus and dependent variable
   c. experimental stimulus and placebo

d. placebo and dependent variable

e. experimental stimulus and independent variable

7. Professor Riley performed an experiment in which neither the subjects nor the experimenter knew who got the stimulus. This is an example of which type of experiment?
   a. one-shot case study
   b. classical design
   c. double-blind experiment
   d. static-group comparison
   e. pretest-posttest design

8. Matching refers to
   a. linking subjects in the pretest group with those in the posttest group
   b. selecting pairs of subjects who are included and not included in an experiment
   c. selecting similar pairs and assigning each member randomly to the experimental and control groups
   d. linking pairs on the independent variable with those on the dependent variable
   e. assigning similar pairs to different settings for the same experiment

9. Reporter Stocker is involved in testing the effects of watching the news on the emotional health of young children. She decides to use a class of Montessori children and a class of public school elementary children as her experimental and control groups. This is an example of which type of experiment?
   a. double-blind experiment
   b. static-group comparison
   c. classical design
   d. posttest-only control group design
   e. one-shot case study

10. Professor Flynn performed an experiment on the effects of interpersonal attraction on conflict orientation, but he used different measures of conflict orientation at the pretest and posttest. Which problem of internal validity does this example reflect?
    a. selection bias
    b. testing
    c. experimental mortality

d.   maturation

e.   instrumentation

11. Elmer, a subject in Professor Jencken's experiment testing the effects of certain films on a person's emotional state, has just undergone a break-up with his girlfriend. He continues with the experiment, however. Which one of the following threatens internal validity?

a.   history

b.   maturation

c.   selection biases

d.   selection maturation

e.   experimental mortality

12. Professor Holstege conducted an experiment on the effects of lawyer volunteers on parole violations. Those parolees with access to lawyer volunteers had fewer parole violations than those without, but the control group parolees felt left out and committed more crimes as a result. Which problem of invalidity does this example reflect?

a.   compensatory rivalry

b.   imitation of treatments

c.   causal time-order

d.   demoralization

e.   selection biases

13. External invalidity refers to problems with

a.   randomization into experimental and control groups

b.   generalizability

c.   assessing ethical violations

d.   assessing posttest effects

e.   selection

14. What is the basic difference between the classical design and the Solomon four-group design?

a.   there is no difference

b.   more time between stimulus and second observation in Solomon four-group

c.   Solomon four-group has randomization

d.   Solomon four-group repeats the classical design but adds groups that are not pretested

e.   Solomon four-group repeats the classical design but adds groups that are not posttested

15. Natural experiments are most likely to resemble which one of the following designs?
    a.   static-group comparison
    b.   classical
    c.   Solomon four-group
    d.   one-group pretest-posttest
    e.   posttest-only control group design

DISCUSSION QUESTIONS

1. Describe the classical experiment. Explain the importance of each of the three major pairs of components.

2. Compare and contrast the three basic strategies for making the subjects in the experimental and control groups as similar as possible. Which one is best? Why? Which technique is actually used most frequently? Why?

3. Differentiate internal from external invalidity. Describe at least two factors contributing to each. Which one of the two—internal or external invalidity—is more serious? Why?

4. Which features of the classical experimental design would be most difficult to incorporate in a natural experiment? Why?

EXERCISE 9.1

Your assignment is to design a small-group experiment that would test the following hypothesis using the classical design:

Despite the negative image men frequently have of women's analytical abilities, those men who work with women that appear clearly more effective than themselves in finding a solution to a problem-solving task will have a higher regard for women than men who do not have such an experience.

1. Describe the experimental and control groups appropriate to the experiment. Describe how you would select people for the study. Describe how you would assign people to the experimental and control groups.

2. Describe a problem-solving task that might be appropriate for this experiment. That is, develop a problem-solving task that would offer the subjects the experience of seeing women do better than men.

3. Describe the means by which you would test the attitudes of men regarding women's analytical abilities prior to the experiment (pretest of attitudes).

4. Describe how you would make sure that the women in the problem-solving groups would be clearly more effective in solving the problem than the men.

5. Describe the means by which you would test the attitudes of men regarding women's analytical abilities after the problem-solving exercises (posttest of attitudes).

6. Describe some of the potential sources of internal invalidity that your design reduces or avoids. Explain why or how your design does this.

7. Describe some of the potential sources of external invalidity that your design reduces or avoids. Explain why or how your design does this.

8. Make up some "results" that you might get in such an experiment and interpret them. Be sure to indicate whether the "results" tend to confirm or disconfirm the hypothesis.

EXERCISE 9.2

Your assignment is to conduct an experiment on your friends and acquaintances, aimed at testing their sincerity in asking and answering the question, "How are you?"

Your experiment will involve three groups of six subjects each: a control group and two experimental groups. Subjects will be placed in the groups as follows.

CONTROL GROUP: As you meet friends over the course of a few days, you are to greet six of them by saying, "Hi, how are you?" Record exactly how they answer.

EXPERIMENTAL GROUP 1: For six other friends, allow them to ask how you are first, and reply by saying, "Great, how are you?" Record exactly how they answer.

EXPERIMENTAL GROUP 2: For six other friends, allow them to ask how you are first, and reply by saying, "Terrible, how are you?" Record exactly how they answer.

In assigning friends to the two experimental groups, be sure to alternate "great" and "terrible," saying "great" to one and "terrible" to the next, and so forth. Get people into the control group whenever you are able to beat them to the punch.

1. Responses given by subjects in the control group:

1. _____

2. _____

3. _____

4. _____

5. _____

6. _____

2. Responses given by subjects in Experimental Group 1 ("Great, how are you?"):

    1. _____

    2. _____

    3. _____

    4. _____

    5. _____

    6. _____

3. Responses given by subjects in Experimental Group 2 ("Terrible, how are you?"):

    1. _____

    2. _____

    3. _____

    4. _____

    5. _____

    6. _____

4. Score each of the responses as "positive," "neutral," or "negative." For example, a subject who answered "great" would be scored as "positive," one who answered "lousy" would be scored as "negative," and one who answered "so-so" would be scored as "neutral." Your task is to figure out the proper scoring for other kinds of responses. Go back to your answers above and write "positive," "neutral," or "negative" beside each of the responses. Describe any difficulties you experienced in coding answers.

5. Complete the table below, entering the percentages of "positive," "neutral," and "negative" responses received from each of the three groups.

	Control Group	Experimental Group 1	Experimental Group 2
Percent positive	_____	_____	_____
Percent neutral	_____	_____	_____
Percent negative	_____	_____	_____
	100% (6)	100% (6)	100% (6)

6. Provide a brief interpretation of your research findings.

7. Describe the success or failure you experienced in assigning people randomly to the groups.

8. Assess this design in terms of sources of internal invalidity.

9. Assess this design in terms of sources of external invalidity.

EXERCISE 9.3

You have been asked to develop a study of the effects of watching *Sesame Street* on children's sex-role orientations, intelligence, or sociability. Describe how you would design the study using a preexperimental design (one-shot case study, one-group pretest-posttest design, static-group comparison). Describe how you would design the study using a true experimental design (classical design, Solomon four-group design, posttest-only control group design). Note the major advantage and weakness of each design.

Chapter 10

Survey Research

OBJECTIVES

1. Illustrate how surveys may be used for descriptive, explanatory, and exploratory purposes.

2. List three methods for distributing self-administered questionnaires.

3. List three principles for mail distribution and return of questionnaires.

4. Present an argument for monitoring returns, and show how this can be done with the return rate graph.

5. List three principles regarding follow-up mailings.

6. State the response rates that Babbie considers adequate, good, and very good.

7. Present four advantages of interviews over questionnaires.

8. Restate the five general rules for successful interviewing.

9. Discuss the role of specifications in training interviewers.

10. List five advantages and three problems with telephone surveys.

11. Show how random-digit dialing and computer-assisted telephone interviewing overcome some of the weaknesses of the telephone survey.

12. Contrast questionnaires and interviews, and describe when each is most appropriate.

13. Assess the strengths and weaknesses of survey design.

14. Give two examples of secondary analysis and/or data archives, and summarize the advantages and disadvantages of this approach.

SUMMARY

Survey research is the most frequently used mode of gathering data in the social sciences. It consists of selecting a sample of respondents and administering a questionnaire or an interview to them. Surveys may be used for descriptive, explanatory, and exploratory purposes. The unit of analysis is usually the individual, but surveys can be used for other units of analysis as well. Survey research is particularly well suited for studying attitudes and orientations in a large population.

Self-administered questionnaires are generally executed by mail, although sometimes they are administered to a group of respondents, and sometimes they are delivered and picked up at a later time. Self-mailing questionnaires require no return envelopes, making it easier to return the instrument. Questionnaires can be sent via first-class postage or bulk rate and returned via postage stamps or business-reply permits. When each option would be used is determined largely by the budget and the expected return rate.

Monitoring the returns of questionnaires is an important part of the study and can be accomplished with a return rate graph plotting the number of questionnaires returned each day. Such a graph can provide clues about when follow-up mailings should occur, and it may be useful in estimating nonresponse bias. Follow-up mailings may contain only a letter of additional encouragement or may contain a new copy of the questionnaire as well. Follow-up mailings significantly increase return rates; two follow-ups mailed two or three weeks apart are best.

There are no strict standards for determining an acceptable response rate. High response rates increase the probability that the respondents accurately represent the sample, thus reducing the chance of response bias. But a demonstrated lack of response bias is more crucial than the response rate itself. A response rate of at least 50 percent is adequate, 60 percent is considered good, and 70 percent is considered very good.

Interviews provide a number of advantages over the self-administered questionnaire. They attain higher response rates, decrease the number of "don't know" and "no answer" responses, help correct confusing items, and provide the opportunity to observe the social situation as well as to ask questions.

It is critical that the interviewer serve as a neutral conduit through which questions and answers are transmitted. Interviewers should have a pleasant demeanor and dress in a fashion similar to the people being interviewed. Familiarity with the instrument will lessen the time required and minimize problems with individual items. Interviewers should follow the question wording exactly and record responses exactly.

One particular skill required is probing, whereby the interviewer redirects inappropriate answers while maintaining the neutral role. When multiple interviewers are employed, the researcher should thoroughly train and supervise the interviewers. Researchers should also prepare specifications, which are explanatory and clarifying comments about handling difficult or confusing situations that may arise with a specific item.

Telephone surveys save money and time, sometimes enhance willingness to give socially disapproved answers, and yield greater control when several interviewers are employed. They also alleviate personal safety concerns. But they come with several problems. They have a bad reputation, for example, and people can hang up easily before the interview is completed. Computer-assisted telephone interviewing is frequently used with random-digit dialing to enhance the reliability and validity of the results. Computer-assisted survey methods are also increasingly being used for in-person interviews.

Self-administered questionnaires and interviews each have advantages and disadvantages. Questionnaires are generally cheaper and quicker and are more appropriate in dealing with more sensitive issues. Interviews help reduce incomplete answers, are more effective in dealing with complicated issues, enable a researcher to conduct a survey based only on a sample of addresses, and provide the opportunity to make important observations apart from the responses to the items. Interviews generally yield higher response rates.

The survey design itself has strengths and weaknesses compared to other designs. It is particularly appropriate for describing the characteristics of large populations, thereby making large samples feasible. In some respects, surveys are quite flexible, and the use of standardized questions enhances reliability. But these advantages come at some cost. Standardization often results in overlooking other appropriate responses and may generate inflexibility in modifying questions. Surveys seldom analyze the context of social life. They are frequently labeled as artificial because the topic of study may not be amenable to measurement through questionnaires, and the act of studying that topic may affect the results. In short, survey research is weak on validity and strong on reliability.

Researchers with a need for survey data cannot always afford to conduct large-scale surveys themselves. Hence many researchers employ secondary analysis of data gathered for some other purpose. Such research has experienced increased popularity due to the establishment of data archives, research centers that collect and distribute many different types of data sets. Such analysis can be done quite rapidly and inexpensively. The key problem with secondary analysis is validity; when one researcher collects data for a given purpose, other researchers have no assurance that such data will be appropriate for their research interests. Comparability of measures is a particular problem.

TERMS

1. computer-assisted telephone interviewing (CATI)
2. data archive
3. interview
4. probe
5. random-digit dialing
6. response rate
7. return rate graph
8. secondary analysis
9. self-administered questionnaire
10. self-mailing questionnaire
11. specifications
12. survey
13. telephone poll

MATCHING

____ 1. A method of data gathering in which a sample of respondents is administered a questionnaire.

____ 2. Questionnaires that require no return postage.

_____ 3. Collections of data sets gathered and administered by research consortiums.

_____ 4. A method that helps the researcher keep track of the progress of data collection.

_____ 5. A strategy used in telephone interviews to eliminate the problem of unlisted numbers.

_____ 6. Explanatory and clarifying comments about the handling of difficult or confusing situations that may occur in an interview situation.

_____ 7. A method used by interviewers to obtain elaboration of respondents' answers to open-ended questions.

_____ 8. A method of research in which researchers analyze data that another researcher has collected.

REVIEW QUESTIONS

1. Which of the following research methods is most often found in sociological journals?
   a. survey research
   b. exploratory research
   c. experimental research
   d. field research
   e. evaluation research

2. A particularly useful strategy for improving response rates to self-administered questionnaires is to
   a. offer an inducement
   b. use commemorative stamps
   c. use colored paper
   d. use hand delivery and/or pick up
   e. use a jazzy cover letter

3. An important feature of using a return rate graph is to
   a. reduce sampling error
   b. examine history effects

151

c. examine measurement effects
d. estimate nonresponse biases
e. improve reliability

4. According to Babbie, which one of the following follow-up procedures is most efficient in getting a high response rate?
   a. an original and then a follow-up letter
   b. an original only
   c. an original and two follow-ups
   d. an original with one follow-up letter and questionnaire
   e. none of the above

5. According to Babbie, a 60 percent return rate is considered
   a. poor
   b. adequate
   c. good
   d. very good
   e. excellent

6. Which one of the following is *not* an advantage of interviews over questionnaires?
   a. increased response rates
   b. safeguard against confusing items
   c. lower numbers of "don't know" and "no answer" responses
   d. increased reliability
   e. all are advantages

7. Which one of the following is *not* a good suggestion for conducting interviews?
   a. follow question wording exactly
   b. dress in your best dress clothes
   c. probe for responses
   d. record responses exactly
   e. all are good suggestions

8. Interviewers can be helped in dealing with confusing situations regarding a given item through the use of clarifying comments known as
   a. specifications
   b. elaborations
   c. matrix questions

d.   response set formats

e.   conversations

9   Which one of the following is *false* regarding telephone interviews?
   a.   they are cheaper than in-person interviews
   b.   they save time over in-person interviews
   c.   they enhance the safety of the interviewer
   d.   they make it harder for the respondent to terminate the interview
   e.   they have a bad reputation

10.   Random-digit dialing *best* addresses which problem in telephone surveys?
   a.   missing data on some items
   b.   sampling frame problems
   c.   the time it takes to do all the dialing
   d.   confidence intervals
   e.   having people hang up

11.   Which is *not* an advantage of survey research?
   a.   increased validity
   b.   increased reliability
   c.   increased generalizability
   d.   increased flexibility in analysis
   e.   feasibility of larger samples

12.   The major problem with secondary analysis pertains to
   a.   theory
   b.   hypotheses
   c.   validity
   d.   sampling
   e.   empirical generalization

DISCUSSION QUESTIONS

1.   Why is a low response rate of concern in survey research? Why is response bias of concern? Which is a more serious threat to survey results and generalization--low response rates or response biases? Why?

2. Compare and contrast interviews and questionnaires on the several dimensions noted in the chapter.

3. Write a first draft of a brief guide for new interviewers.

4. Compare the strengths and weaknesses of surveys and experiments.

EXERCISE 10.1

Use the information that follows to construct both types of return rate graphs that Babbie discusses. Then write a short analysis of the results.

A questionnaire was mailed to 1,000 students (both off-campus and on-campus) at Northern Michigan University on March 1. A follow-up was done on March 17. The questionnaires were returned as follows:

Date	# Received	Date	# Received
March 6	2	March 26	no mail
March 7	5	March 27	no mail
March 8	18	March 28	28
March 9	32	March 29	21
March 10	35	March 30	23
March 11	25	March 31	14
March 12	no mail	April 1	12
March 13	no mail	April 2	no mail
March 14	20	April 3	no mail
March 15	19	April 4	10
March 16	20	April 5	11
March 17	14	April 6	9
March 18	13	April 7	6
March 19	no mail	April 8	5
March 20	no mail	April 9	no mail
March 21	16	April 10	no mail
March 22	26	April 11	2
March 23	37	April 12	0
March 24	41		
March 25	30		

1. Create a graph that plots the number of questionnaires returned each day.

2. Create a graph that plots the cumulative number and percentage of questionnaires returned.

3. Summarize the results of both graphs.

EXERCISE 10.2

On the following pages are ten copies of a short interview schedule. Your assignment is to select and interview ten people: five men and five women (your instructor may provide additional sampling instructions). Please be sure to actually interview the respondents; do *not* have them fill out their own questionnaires.

Be sure you complete discussion question #3 before doing this assignment, even if your instructor has not previously required this. After completing the interviews, write a short report of your experiences below. Discuss the problems you experienced and how you dealt with them. Which types of probes did you employ? With what success? Which aspects of the advice for interviewing found in the chapter proved to be the most useful? Which proved to be the least useful? What would you do differently now? Why? How?

Case ID_____   Respondent's sex: [ ] Male [ ] Female

Hello. My name is _____ and I'm conducting a short survey as part of an exercise for my research methods class. Would you be willing to participate in the study? The interview will take less than five minutes. (ENCOURAGE IF RELUCTANT.)

I'm going to read some opinions about the effects of looking at or reading sexual materials. As I read each one, please tell me if you think sexual materials do or do not have that effect. (READ EACH ITEM AND CHECK THE APPROPRIATE CATEGORY.)

	Yes	No	Don't Know	No Answer
1. Sexual materials provide information about sex.	[ ]	[ ]	[ ]	[ ]
2. Sexual materials lead to a breakdown of morals.	[ ]	[ ]	[ ]	[ ]
3. Sexual materials lead people to commit rape.	[ ]	[ ]	[ ]	[ ]
4. Sexual materials provide an outlet for bottled-up impulses.	[ ]	[ ]	[ ]	[ ]

I am going to name some institutions in this country. As far as the PEOPLE RUNNING these institutions are concerned, would you say that you have a great deal of confidence, only some confidence, or hardly any confidence at all in them? (CODE FOR EACH ITEM; CODE DK FOR "DON'T KNOW" OR NA FOR "NO ANSWER" IF APPROPRIATE.)

	Great Deal	Only Some	Hardly Any	DK	NA
5. Education	[ ]	[ ]	[ ]	[ ]	[ ]
6. Press	[ ]	[ ]	[ ]	[ ]	[ ]
7. Congress	[ ]	[ ]	[ ]	[ ]	[ ]

8. Could you tell me, in your own words, how you feel about the "Women's Liberation Movement"?

That completes the interview. Thank you for your cooperation.

Case ID_____   Respondent's sex: [ ] Male [ ] Female

Hello. My name is _____ and I'm conducting a short survey as part of an exercise for my research methods class. Would you be willing to participate in the study? The interview will take less than five minutes. (ENCOURAGE IF RELUCTANT.)

I'm going to read some opinions about the effects of looking at or reading sexual materials. As I read each one, please tell me if you think sexual materials do or do not have that effect. (READ EACH ITEM AND CHECK THE APPROPRIATE CATEGORY.)

	Yes	No	Don't Know	No Answer
1. Sexual materials provide information about sex.	[ ]	[ ]	[ ]	[ ]
2. Sexual materials lead to a breakdown of morals.	[ ]	[ ]	[ ]	[ ]
3. Sexual materials lead people to commit rape.	[ ]	[ ]	[ ]	[ ]
4. Sexual materials provide an outlet for bottled-up impulses.	[ ]	[ ]	[ ]	[ ]

I am going to name some institutions in this country. As far as the PEOPLE RUNNING these institutions are concerned, would you say that you have a great deal of confidence, only some confidence, or hardly any confidence at all in them? (CODE FOR EACH ITEM; CODE DK FOR "DON'T KNOW" OR NA FOR "NO ANSWER" IF APPROPRIATE.)

	Great Deal	Only Some	Hardly Any	DK	NA
5. Education	[ ]	[ ]	[ ]	[ ]	[ ]
6. Press	[ ]	[ ]	[ ]	[ ]	[ ]
7. Congress	[ ]	[ ]	[ ]	[ ]	[ ]

8. Could you tell me, in your own words, how you feel about the "Women's Liberation Movement"?

That completes the interview. Thank you for your cooperation.

Case ID_____   Respondent's sex: [ ] Male   [ ] Female

Hello. My name is _____ and I'm conducting a short survey as part of an exercise for my research methods class. Would you be willing to participate in the study? The interview will take less than five minutes. (ENCOURAGE IF RELUCTANT.)

I'm going to read some opinions about the effects of looking at or reading sexual materials. As I read each one, please tell me if you think sexual materials do or do not have that effect. (READ EACH ITEM AND CHECK THE APPROPRIATE CATEGORY.)

	Yes	No	Don't Know	No Answer
1. Sexual materials provide information about sex.	[ ]	[ ]	[ ]	[ ]
2. Sexual materials lead to a breakdown of morals.	[ ]	[ ]	[ ]	[ ]
3. Sexual materials lead people to commit rape.	[ ]	[ ]	[ ]	[ ]
4. Sexual materials provide an outlet for bottled-up impulses.	[ ]	[ ]	[ ]	[ ]

I am going to name some institutions in this country. As far as the PEOPLE RUNNING these institutions are concerned, would you say that you have a great deal of confidence, only some confidence, or hardly any confidence at all in them? (CODE FOR EACH ITEM; CODE DK FOR "DON'T KNOW" OR NA FOR "NO ANSWER" IF APPROPRIATE.)

	Great Deal	Only Some	Hardly Any	DK	NA
5. Education	[ ]	[ ]	[ ]	[ ]	[ ]
6. Press	[ ]	[ ]	[ ]	[ ]	[ ]
7. Congress	[ ]	[ ]	[ ]	[ ]	[ ]

8. Could you tell me, in your own words, how you feel about the "Women's Liberation Movement"?

That completes the interview. Thank you for your cooperation.

Case ID_____   Respondent's sex: [ ] Male [ ] Female

Hello. My name is _____ and I'm conducting a short survey as part of an exercise for my research methods class. Would you be willing to participate in the study? The interview will take less than five minutes. (ENCOURAGE IF RELUCTANT.)

I'm going to read some opinions about the effects of looking at or reading sexual materials. As I read each one, please tell me if you think sexual materials do or do not have that effect. (READ EACH ITEM AND CHECK THE APPROPRIATE CATEGORY.)

	Yes	No	Don't Know	No Answer
1. Sexual materials provide information about sex.	[ ]	[ ]	[ ]	[ ]
2. Sexual materials lead to a breakdown of morals.	[ ]	[ ]	[ ]	[ ]
3. Sexual materials lead people to commit rape.	[ ]	[ ]	[ ]	[ ]
4. Sexual materials provide an outlet for bottled-up impulses.	[ ]	[ ]	[ ]	[ ]

I am going to name some institutions in this country. As far as the PEOPLE RUNNING these institutions are concerned, would you say that you have a great deal of confidence, only some confidence, or hardly any confidence at all in them? (CODE FOR EACH ITEM; CODE DK FOR "DON'T KNOW" OR NA FOR "NO ANSWER" IF APPROPRIATE.)

	Great Deal	Only Some	Hardly Any	DK	NA
5. Education	[ ]	[ ]	[ ]	[ ]	[ ]
6. Press	[ ]	[ ]	[ ]	[ ]	[ ]
7. Congress	[ ]	[ ]	[ ]	[ ]	[ ]

8. Could you tell me, in your own words, how you feel about the "Women's Liberation Movement"?

That completes the interview. Thank you for your cooperation.

Case ID_____ Respondent's sex: [ ] Male [ ] Female

Hello. My name is _____ and I'm conducting a short survey as part of an exercise for my research methods class. Would you be willing to participate in the study? The interview will take less than five minutes. (ENCOURAGE IF RELUCTANT.)

I'm going to read some opinions about the effects of looking at or reading sexual materials. As I read each one, please tell me if you think sexual materials do or do not have that effect. (READ EACH ITEM AND CHECK THE APPROPRIATE CATEGORY.)

	Yes	No	Don't Know	No Answer
1. Sexual materials provide information about sex.	[ ]	[ ]	[ ]	[ ]
2. Sexual materials lead to a breakdown of morals.	[ ]	[ ]	[ ]	[ ]
3. Sexual materials lead people to commit rape.	[ ]	[ ]	[ ]	[ ]
4. Sexual materials provide an outlet for bottled-up impulses.	[ ]	[ ]	[ ]	[ ]

I am going to name some institutions in this country. As far as the PEOPLE RUNNING these institutions are concerned, would you say that you have a great deal of confidence, only some confidence, or hardly any confidence at all in them? (CODE FOR EACH ITEM; CODE DK FOR "DON'T KNOW" OR NA FOR "NO ANSWER" IF APPROPRIATE.)

	Great Deal	Only Some	Hardly Any	DK	NA
5. Education	[ ]	[ ]	[ ]	[ ]	[ ]
6. Press	[ ]	[ ]	[ ]	[ ]	[ ]
7. Congress	[ ]	[ ]	[ ]	[ ]	[ ]

8. Could you tell me, in your own words, how you feel about the "Women's Liberation Movement"?

That completes the interview. Thank you for your cooperation.

Case ID_____   Respondent's sex: [ ] Male [ ] Female

Hello. My name is _____ and I'm conducting a short survey as part of an exercise for my research methods class. Would you be willing to participate in the study? The interview will take less than five minutes. (ENCOURAGE IF RELUCTANT.)

I'm going to read some opinions about the effects of looking at or reading sexual materials. As I read each one, please tell me if you think sexual materials do or do not have that effect. (READ EACH ITEM AND CHECK THE APPROPRIATE CATEGORY.)

	Yes	No	Don't Know	No Answer
1. Sexual materials provide information about sex.	[ ]	[ ]	[ ]	[ ]
2. Sexual materials lead to a breakdown of morals.	[ ]	[ ]	[ ]	[ ]
3. Sexual materials lead people to commit rape.	[ ]	[ ]	[ ]	[ ]
4. Sexual materials provide an outlet for bottled-up impulses.	[ ]	[ ]	[ ]	[ ]

I am going to name some institutions in this country. As far as the PEOPLE RUNNING these institutions are concerned, would you say that you have a great deal of confidence, only some confidence, or hardly any confidence at all in them? (CODE FOR EACH ITEM; CODE DK FOR "DON'T KNOW" OR NA FOR "NO ANSWER" IF APPROPRIATE.)

	Great Deal	Only Some	Hardly Any	DK	NA
5. Education	[ ]	[ ]	[ ]	[ ]	[ ]
6. Press	[ ]	[ ]	[ ]	[ ]	[ ]
7. Congress	[ ]	[ ]	[ ]	[ ]	[ ]

8. Could you tell me, in your own words, how you feel about the "Women's Liberation Movement"?

That completes the interview. Thank you for your cooperation.

Case ID_____   Respondent's sex: [ ] Male [ ] Female

Hello. My name is _____ and I'm conducting a short survey as part of an exercise for my research methods class. Would you be willing to participate in the study? The interview will take less than five minutes. (ENCOURAGE IF RELUCTANT.)

I'm going to read some opinions about the effects of looking at or reading sexual materials. As I read each one, please tell me if you think sexual materials do or do not have that effect. (READ EACH ITEM AND CHECK THE APPROPRIATE CATEGORY.)

		Yes	No	Don't Know	No Answer
1.	Sexual materials provide information about sex.	[ ]	[ ]	[ ]	[ ]
2.	Sexual materials lead to a breakdown of morals.	[ ]	[ ]	[ ]	[ ]
3.	Sexual materials lead people to commit rape.	[ ]	[ ]	[ ]	[ ]
4.	Sexual materials provide an outlet for bottled-up impulses.	[ ]	[ ]	[ ]	[ ]

I am going to name some institutions in this country. As far as the PEOPLE RUNNING these institutions are concerned, would you say that you have a great deal of confidence, only some confidence, or hardly any confidence at all in them? (CODE FOR EACH ITEM; CODE DK FOR "DON'T KNOW" OR NA FOR "NO ANSWER" IF APPROPRIATE.)

		Great Deal	Only Some	Hardly Any	DK	NA
5.	Education	[ ]	[ ]	[ ]	[ ]	[ ]
6.	Press	[ ]	[ ]	[ ]	[ ]	[ ]
7.	Congress	[ ]	[ ]	[ ]	[ ]	[ ]

8. Could you tell me, in your own words, how you feel about the "Women's Liberation Movement"?

That completes the interview. Thank you for your cooperation.

Case ID_____   Respondent's sex: [ ] Male [ ] Female

Hello. My name is _____ and I'm conducting a short survey as part of an exercise for my research methods class. Would you be willing to participate in the study? The interview will take less than five minutes. (ENCOURAGE IF RELUCTANT.)

I'm going to read some opinions about the effects of looking at or reading sexual materials. As I read each one, please tell me if you think sexual materials do or do not have that effect. (READ EACH ITEM AND CHECK THE APPROPRIATE CATEGORY.)

	Yes	No	Don't Know	No Answer
1. Sexual materials provide information about sex.	[ ]	[ ]	[ ]	[ ]
2. Sexual materials lead to a breakdown of morals.	[ ]	[ ]	[ ]	[ ]
3. Sexual materials lead people to commit rape.	[ ]	[ ]	[ ]	[ ]
4. Sexual materials provide an outlet for bottled-up impulses.	[ ]	[ ]	[ ]	[ ]

I am going to name some institutions in this country. As far as the PEOPLE RUNNING these institutions are concerned, would you say that you have a great deal of confidence, only some confidence, or hardly any confidence at all in them? (CODE FOR EACH ITEM; CODE DK FOR "DON'T KNOW" OR NA FOR "NO ANSWER" IF APPROPRIATE.)

	Great Deal	Only Some	Hardly Any	DK	NA
5. Education	[ ]	[ ]	[ ]	[ ]	[ ]
6. Press	[ ]	[ ]	[ ]	[ ]	[ ]
7. Congress	[ ]	[ ]	[ ]	[ ]	[ ]

8. Could you tell me, in your own words, how you feel about the "Women's Liberation Movement"?

That completes the interview. Thank you for your cooperation.

Case ID_____   Respondent's sex: [ ] Male [ ] Female

Hello. My name is _____ and I'm conducting a short survey as part of an exercise for my research methods class. Would you be willing to participate in the study? The interview will take less than five minutes. (ENCOURAGE IF RELUCTANT.)

I'm going to read some opinions about the effects of looking at or reading sexual materials. As I read each one, please tell me if you think sexual materials do or do not have that effect. (READ EACH ITEM AND CHECK THE APPROPRIATE CATEGORY.)

	Yes	No	Don't Know	No Answer
1. Sexual materials provide information about sex.	[ ]	[ ]	[ ]	[ ]
2. Sexual materials lead to a breakdown of morals.	[ ]	[ ]	[ ]	[ ]
3. Sexual materials lead people to commit rape.	[ ]	[ ]	[ ]	[ ]
4. Sexual materials provide an outlet for bottled-up impulses.	[ ]	[ ]	[ ]	[ ]

I am going to name some institutions in this country. As far as the PEOPLE RUNNING these institutions are concerned, would you say that you have a great deal of confidence, only some confidence, or hardly any confidence at all in them? (CODE FOR EACH ITEM; CODE DK FOR "DON'T KNOW" OR NA FOR "NO ANSWER" IF APPROPRIATE.)

	Great Deal	Only Some	Hardly Any	DK	NA
5. Education	[ ]	[ ]	[ ]	[ ]	[ ]
6. Press	[ ]	[ ]	[ ]	[ ]	[ ]
7. Congress	[ ]	[ ]	[ ]	[ ]	[ ]

8. Could you tell me, in your own words, how you feel about the "Women's Liberation Movement"?

That completes the interview. Thank you for your cooperation.

Case ID_____   Respondent's sex: [ ] Male [ ] Female

Hello. My name is _____ and I'm conducting a short survey as part of an exercise for my research methods class. Would you be willing to participate in the study? The interview will take less than five minutes. (ENCOURAGE IF RELUCTANT.)

I'm going to read some opinions about the effects of looking at or reading sexual materials. As I read each one, please tell me if you think sexual materials do or do not have that effect. (READ EACH ITEM AND CHECK THE APPROPRIATE CATEGORY.)

	Yes	No	Don't Know	No Answer
1. Sexual materials provide information about sex.	[ ]	[ ]	[ ]	[ ]
2. Sexual materials lead to a breakdown of morals.	[ ]	[ ]	[ ]	[ ]
3. Sexual materials lead people to commit rape.	[ ]	[ ]	[ ]	[ ]
4. Sexual materials provide an outlet for bottled-up impulses.	[ ]	[ ]	[ ]	[ ]

I am going to name some institutions in this country. As far as the PEOPLE RUNNING these institutions are concerned, would you say that you have a great deal of confidence, only some confidence, or hardly any confidence at all in them? (CODE FOR EACH ITEM; CODE DK FOR "DON'T KNOW" OR NA FOR "NO ANSWER" IF APPROPRIATE.)

	Great Deal	Only Some	Hardly Any	DK	NA
5. Education	[ ]	[ ]	[ ]	[ ]	[ ]
6. Press	[ ]	[ ]	[ ]	[ ]	[ ]
7. Congress	[ ]	[ ]	[ ]	[ ]	[ ]

8. Could you tell me, in your own words, how you feel about the "Women's Liberation Movement"?

That completes the interview. Thank you for your cooperation.

Chapter 11

Field Research

OBJECTIVES

1. Summarize the three key strengths of field research.

2. Define and give examples of each of the following types of social phenomena addressed by field researchers: meanings, practices, episodes, encounters, roles, relationships, groups, organizations, and settlements.

3. Give three examples of research topics particularly appropriate for field research.

4. Compare the following four roles that field researchers may play, and give examples of each: complete participant, participant-as-observer, observer-as-participant, and complete observer.

5. Provide advice on each of the following steps in preparing for the field: review of the relevant literature, use of informants, and establishing initial contacts.

6. Explain why sampling in field research is more complicated than in the other types of designs.

7. Show how each of the following sampling designs might be used in field research: quota sample, snowball sample, deviant cases sample, and purposive sample.

8. Provide advice for asking questions in field research, and compare a field research interview with normal conversation.

9. Provide advice for recording observations in field research.

10. Provide advice on data processing in field research, particularly regarding the rewriting of notes and the creation of files.

11. Provide advice on analyzing data in field research.

12. Address the strengths and weaknesses of field research, being certain to compare field research with experiments and surveys in terms of validity, reliability, and generalizability.

SUMMARY

Field research closely parallels our daily observation of and participation in social behavior, as well as our attempt to understand such behavior. The social scientific application of field research requires specific skills and techniques and hence is more useful than casual observation. It is both a data-gathering strategy and a theory-generating activity. Field research is particularly appropriate for topics that appear to defy simple quantification and that require the comprehensiveness of perspective the field researcher can provide. It is also useful for studying topics and people within their natural settings and for investigating social processes over time.

The field researcher may investigate various types of social phenomena. One type is meanings, which include culture and norms. Another is practices, which involve behavior. Episodes refer to specific events. Encounters involve people interacting. Roles include positions and behavior. Another type is relationships, which pertain to behavior found in sets of roles. Groups involve small numbers of interacting people. Organizations are larger than groups. Finally, settlements include small-scale "societies."

The field researcher may play one or more roles. The researcher's identity and purpose are not known to those being observed in the complete participant role. This strategy requires complete adherence to the norms of the group but may involve ethical problems. Also, the researcher may affect what is being studied. The participant-as-observer role involves full participation, but the people being

170

studied know the researcher's identity. As a result, they may alter some of their normal behaviors. The observer-as-participant role requires identification of the researcher role and some interaction with the participants but does not require extensive participation. The researcher playing the complete observer role observes a social situation without becoming a part of it.

Field research follows a logical progression of steps. The researcher must first prepare for the field by examining relevant literature, by using informants to help frame the analysis, and by establishing initial contacts with the people to be studied.

In some respects, field researchers deliberately try to observe everything, thereby precluding sampling. When they do sample, they frequently employ nonprobability sampling strategies. With quota sampling, persons representing different participation categories are studied. With snowball sampling, the researcher uses initial contacts to identify subsequent contacts. With deviant cases sampling, the researcher studies cases that do not fit regular patterns of attitudes and behaviors. With purposive sampling, the researcher selects a sample of observations that are believed to yield the most comprehensive understanding of a subject. Thus, controlled sampling techniques are infrequently used in field research, and the population and units of analysis are not always clear.

When sampling is employed, the field researcher must recognize that the situations available for observation may not be representative of the more general class of phenomena the researcher wishes to describe or explain. Second, the actual observations may not fall within those total situations representative of all the possible observations.

Field researchers typically employ unstructured interviews to ask questions. This conversational approach yields flexibility in that an answer to one question may influence the next question the researcher wishes to ask. Probing is essential.

The field journal contains the field researcher's observations. Field notes should include both empirical observations as well as interpretations, although the observations and interpretations should be kept distinct. Field researchers learn not to trust their memories and hence take many notes at multiple stages in the research process. They record as much as possible so that interpretations that do not seem evident at the time the notes are taken may emerge later.

Data processing requires constant writing and rewriting of notes, preferably in typed form and with several copies. Computers are used to facilitate the transcription and analysis of field notes. Field researchers may then organize their notes into several files, including a chronological record, background files, biographical files, bibliographical files, and analytical files.

It is important to identify similarities and dissimilarities in the data analysis process. Such classifications yield order among all the notes and observations and contribute to the formulation of theoretical propositions and their assessment. Field researchers must be particularly alert to observing only those things that support their theoretical conclusions. This problem may be alleviated by supplementing observations with quantitative data, by involving multiple researchers, and through introspection.

The greatest strength of the field research method is the presence of an observing, thinking researcher on the scene of the action. Field researchers are in a unique position to examine the nuances of attitudes and behaviors and to examine social processes over time; both contribute to a deeper understanding. Field research also is inexpensive and provides a great deal of flexibility for moving between observation and analysis.

However, field research seldom yields descriptive statements about large populations because it is a qualitative rather than a quantitative approach. As a result, the field researcher's conclusions are seen as tentative rather than definitive. Although field research is often more valid than surveys and experiments, it does suffer from low reliability. Finally, generalizability is a problem for field research because replication is difficult, because comprehensiveness comes at the expense of generalizability, and because those observed may not be representative of the remaining group.

TERMS

1. complete observer
2. complete participant
3. deviant cases sample
4. field dilemma
5. field research
6. informants
7. introspection
8. norms

9. observer-as-participant
10. participant-as-observer
11. purposive sampling
12. qualitative research
13. quota sampling
14. snowball sample
15. universals
16. unstructured interview

MATCHING

____ 1. The researcher role in which researchers identify themselves as researchers and interact with the participants while making no pretense about actually being a participant.

____ 2. A sampling procedure whereby persons representing all different participation categories are studied.

____ 3. A sampling procedure whereby cases that do not fit into regular patterns are studied.

____ 4. An interaction between a researcher and a respondent in which the interviewer has a general plan of inquiry but not a specific set of questions that must be asked in particular words or in a particular order.

____ 5. The process of interpreting social behavior through one's own "glasses."

____ 6. The omission of information that may be helpful in making sound conclusions.

____ 7. A researcher role in which the researcher participates fully with the group under study but makes it clear that he or she is also undertaking research.

____ 8. The process of examining one's own thoughts and feelings used to understand the world around oneself.

REVIEW QUESTIONS

1. Field research differs from other modes of observation in that
   a. it is more highly refined
   b. it is both a data-collecting activity and a theory-generating activity
   c. it involves more careful conceptualization and operationalization
   d. it is more dependent on using deduction to generate specific hypotheses for testing
   e. it is more reliable and valid

2. Professor Sullivan performed an observational study of the norms that govern interactions between cab drivers and their passengers. Which one of the following does this example reflect?
   a. meanings
   b. practices
   c. episodes
   d. groups
   e. settlements

3. Professor Mallory did a field research study of teacher-student interactions by sitting in the back of classrooms. She occasionally helped students when they were doing work at their desks. Which role was she playing?
   a. complete participant
   b. participant-as-observer
   c. observer-as-participant
   d. complete observer
   e. ethnographer

4. The most serious ethical problems exist for which type of research role?
   a. complete participant
   b. participant-as-observer
   c. observer-as-participant
   d. complete observer
   e. ethnographer

5. A common first step in doing field research is
   a. considering ethics
   b. forming a hypothesis
   c. constructing a theory
   d. deciding on level of participation
   e. reviewing literature

6. A major reason why controlled sampling techniques are seldom used in field research is that
   a. too few people are studied
   b. the unit of analysis and the population are not always clear
   c. the social situation is too fluid
   d. the populations do not meet the criteria for calculating sampling error
   e. grounded theory is not possible with such sampling

7. Field researchers who were particularly concerned with representativeness would employ
   a. snowball designs
   b. quota designs
   c. purposive designs
   d. convenience designs
   e. weighting

8. The most appropriate sampling design for studying a loosely structured political group would be
   a. random
   b. quota
   c. snowball
   d. systematic
   e. stratified

9. Which one of the following is most appropriate for asking questions during field research?
   a. structured questionnaire
   b. unstructured questionnaire
   c. structured interviews
   d. unstructured interviews
   e. projective techniques

10. Which one of the following is *false* regarding field notes?
    a. don't trust your memory more than you have to
    b. take notes in stages
    c. get the major points, but don't worry about getting as many details as you can
    d. rewrite your notes before going to sleep
    e. all are true

11. The field researcher should create all *but* which one of the following types of files?
    a. background
    b. event
    c. biographical
    d. bibliographical
    e. analytical

12. Professor Johnson just finished a field research study of skid row residents. The best advice you could give him regarding data analysis would be to examine
    a. similarities and dissimilarities
    b. units of analysis and populations
    c. events and people
    d. chronology and meaning
    e. social relations

13. In comparison to surveys and experiments, field research has
    a. high validity and high reliability
    b. high validity and low reliability
    c. low validity and low reliability
    d. low validity and high reliability
    e. high reliability, but only when the validity is high

14. Generalizability in field research crops up in all *but* which of the following forms?
    a. the observation depends on the particular observer
    b. the comprehensiveness of the research
    c. those observed may not be typical of all members
    d. the adequacy of the measures in reflecting the concepts
    e. they all crop up

DISCUSSION QUESTIONS

1. Explain what Babbie means when he says that field research is not only a data-gathering activity but a theory-generating activity as well. Illustrate each function. Which is more important? Why?

2. Compare and contrast the four roles of the field observer. Select a topic not used in the chapter and show how this topic would be studied from each of the four roles. Which of the four roles would be best for the topic you selected? Why?

3. Babbie discusses the following stages in field research: preparation for the field, sampling, asking questions, recording observations, data processing, and data analysis/drawing conclusions. Select three and discuss the basic principles involved for effectively completing each.

4. Compare the strengths and weaknesses of field research with both surveys and experiments, particularly in terms of reliability and validity.

EXERCISE 11.1

Your assignment is to observe and understand the social dynamics of jaywalking--defined narrowly for our purposes as "pedestrians crossing the street against the light at intersections."

You are to make three separate observations of at least 20 minutes duration each.

Your specific tasks are to discover:

1. What kinds of people are the most likely to jaywalk and what kinds are the least likely to jaywalk?

2. What kinds of people are likely to stimulate jaywalking by others? What kinds of people, when they jaywalk, seem to be followed by those people who were previously waiting for the light to change?

The space below is divided into two sections. The first is for your field notes, and the second is for your research conclusions. Make sure that the two sections are not identical. The first should contain your notes on the observations as you made them, and the second should reflect your analysis of the data (see Chapter 11 on these two tasks).

Please don't get arrested for jaywalking!

FIELD NOTES:

RESEARCH CONCLUSIONS:

EXERCISE 11.2

Your assignment is to pick some location or situation in which strangers are put in physical proximity to one another for a period of time. Examples include a bus stop, a table at the library, a train station or airport waiting room, a hospital waiting room, a party, etc.

Observe at your location for at least an hour. Examine the ways in which strangers interact with one another. Notice the ways in which they communicate: through words, facial expressions, body postures, and the like. Examine what is communicated, in what situations, with what effect, and by what kinds of people. Examine also the importance of social space and physical space. Pay special attention to (a) the varieties in all these things, and (b) any regular patterns that seem to exist.

The space below is divided into two sections. The first is for your field notes, and the second is for your research conclusions. Make sure that the two sections are not identical. The first should contain your notes on the observations as you made them, and the second should reflect your analysis of the data (see Chapter 11 on these two tasks).

FIELD NOTES:

RESEARCH CONCLUSIONS:

EXERCISE 11.3

Your assignment is to plan a possible field research project to investigate differences in friendship patterns in coed and single-sex residence halls. The questions below deal with some of the concepts you may wish to consider in such a study. For each, describe some of the possible indicators that might be relevant to the concept.

1. How would you determine the number of friendships?

2. How would you determine the quality of friendships?

3. Which other aspects of friendship patterns would you expect to differ in the two situations? List at least three along with possible indicators.

4. List two other variables that you might consider in a study such as this.

5. Describe how you might measure the first variable above.

6. Describe how you might measure the second variable above.

Chapter 12

Unobtrusive Research

OBJECTIVES

1. Describe and compare the three unobtrusive research designs: content analysis, analysis of existing statistics, and historical/comparative analysis.

2. Give three examples of artifacts that content analysts might study.

3. Give three examples of content analysis in which the unit of observation differs from the unit of analysis.

4. Show how the unit of analysis influences sample selection in content analysis.

5. Illustrate how a researcher might employ each of the following sampling techniques in content analysis: simple random sampling, systematic sampling, stratified sampling, and cluster sampling.

6. Differentiate manifest content from latent content by definition and example.

7. Present advice for the development of code categories in content analysis.

8. Present advice for counting and record keeping in content analysis.

9. Outline the strengths and weaknesses of content analysis.

10. Summarize the difficulties with units of analysis in existing statistics.

11. Explain why validity is a problem with existing statistics, and present two strategies for resolving this problem.

12. Explain why reliability is a problem with existing statistics, and present two strategies for resolving this problem.

13. List three sources of existing statistics.

14. List three sources of data for historical/comparative analysis.

15. Discuss the role of corroboration in enhancing the quality of existing statistics.

16. Discuss the role of hermeneutics, verstehen, and ideal types in the analysis of existing statistics.

SUMMARY

Unlike other methods, unobtrusive methods do not generally influence the data gathered. Content analysis is one type of unobtrusive method. It may be applied to virtually any form of communication and involves examining artifacts to answer the classic question: "Who says what, to whom, how, and with what effect?"

The complexity of units of analysis is very apparent in content analysis, particularly when the unit of observation differs from the unit of analysis. Content analysts must address this issue directly because sample selection depends largely on the unit of analysis. Any of the conventional sampling techniques described in Chapter 8 may be employed in content analysis, including random or systematic sampling, stratified sampling, and cluster sampling. Sampling need not end when the researcher reaches the unit of analysis.

Content analysts distinguish manifest from latent content. Manifest content is the visible surface content, and its coding approximates the use of a standardized questionnaire. Latent content reflects the underlying meaning, but this advantage comes at a cost of reliability and specificity. It is best to code both types.

Conceptualization plays a key role in determining code categories and frequently requires both inductive and deductive methods. Attributes of variables must be clearly specified, and each of the several levels of measurement may be employed. Pretesting will enhance the conceptualization of content categories. The final product must be numerical, and the base from which counting is done must be carefully considered and must be presented.

The greatest advantage of content analysis is economy in terms of time and energy. Content analysis is also quite safe—mistakes can be easily rectified and the study redone. Content analysis also allows the study of processes over time. But it is limited to an examination of recorded communications, which raises questions regarding validity.

Many governmental and other agencies collect official or quasi-official statistics. Existing statistics can provide the main data for a social scientific study and can also provide supplemental sources of data for studies employing other research designs. The unit of analysis is frequently not the individual but instead is found in different types of aggregates. The aggregate nature of existing statistics sometimes presents a problem, requiring the social scientist to make inferences from one level to another. Doing so, however, may result in committing the ecological fallacy—generalizing from data gathered at one unit of analysis to another unit of analysis.

Existing statistics are particularly prone to problems of validity because the data may not reflect a particular measure that a social scientist has constructed. This problem may be addressed through logical reasoning and replication. Reliability may also be a problem because different agencies use different data-gathering strategies with varying levels of accuracy. This problem may be addressed through awareness and logical reasoning, as well as replication. There are many sources of existing statistics, such as *The Statistical Abstract of the United States* and *The Demographic Yearbook*.

Historical/comparative research helps trace the development of social forms over time and helps compare such developments across cultures. In its purest form, this approach relies on "primary sources" of data, such as diaries and official government documents. Once again, problems of reliability and bias enter, which again can be addressed through replication (known as corroboration in historical research). Analysts in this tradition often stress the role of verstehen, an understanding of the essential quality of a social phenomenon. Social scientists in this tradition also employ hermeneutics—the art, science, or skill of interpretation. Finding patterns among details sometimes results in the essential characteristics of a social phenomenon. Historical/comparative research is often performed in light of a particular theoretical paradigm, such as Marxism.

TERMS

1. analysis of existing statistics
2. coding
3. content analysis
4. corroboration
5. ecological fallacy
6. hermeneutics
7. historical/comparative analysis
8. ideal types
9. latent content
10. manifest content
11. unobtrusive measures
12. verstehen

MATCHING

____ 1. A research method in which a class of social artifacts is analyzed.

____ 2. The visible, surface content of a communication.

____ 3. The underlying meaning of a communication.

____ 4. This occurs when a researcher gathers data from groups and generalizes to individuals.

____ 5. In historical research the process by which several sources point to the same set of "facts."

____ 6. Research methods that allow the researcher to study social life from afar, without influencing it in the process.

____ 7. Experiential understanding of social life.

____ 8. Conceptual models composed of the essential characteristics of social phenomena.

REVIEW QUESTIONS

1. Content analysis may be applied to
   a. anything that is written
   b. any form of communication
   c. anything social scientific that does not involve surveys, experiments, or observation
   d. anything that has both manifest and latent content
   e. anything that involves statistics

2. Sampling and data analysis are generally more complex in content analysis because
   a. the method is less highly developed than other modes of observation
   b. both sampling and data analysis are not as appropriate
   c. sampling error cannot be calculated
   d. current statistical techniques do not apply
   e. the units of analysis are not always clear

3. Which of the following sampling techniques is/are applicable in content analysis?
   a. simple random
   b. systematic
   c. stratified
   d. purposive
   e. all of the above

4. Professor Hague codes the number of times the word sex is used in commercials. She is examining
   a. latent structure
   b. ecological fallacy
   c. manifest content
   d. corroboration
   e. latent content

5. Professor Spykes codes the frequency that sex is a part of situation comedies. He is examining
   a. latent structure
   b. sociometric choices
   c. manifest content

d. corroboration
e. latent content

6. Which one of the following is *not* a strength of content analysis?
    a. economy in time and money
    b. flexibility and safety
    c. allows study of process over time
    d. unobtrusive
    e. all are strengths

7. In studying suicide, Durkheim used
    a. surveys
    b. experiments
    c. observation
    d. government statistics
    e. evaluation research

8. Durkheim concluded that suicides are a product of
    a. social instability and disintegration
    b. temperature and population density
    c. political party structure
    d. education and family structure
    e. depression

9. The most common unit of analysis involved in the analysis of existing statistics is
    a. individuals
    b. groups
    c. organizations
    d. artifacts
    e. cities

10. Because most existing statistics are aggregated, researchers must avoid the error of
    a. overgeneralizing
    b. validity
    c. drawing conclusions about individuals
    d. drawing conclusions about the aggregate
    e. reductionism

11. The *major* disadvantage of analyzing existing data is
    a. ethical violations
    b. errors in coding
    c. inappropriate statistical techniques
    d. reliability of measures
    e. validity of measures

12. The two features of science used to handle the problem of validity in analysis of existing statistics are
    a. cumulativeness and generalizability
    b. generalizability and objectivity
    c. objectivity and replication
    d. replication and logical reasoning
    e. logical reasoning and cumulativeness

13. One of the most valuable sources of existing statistics is
    a. *Statistical Abstract of the United States*
    b. Superintendent of Documents
    c. *Demographic Yearbook*
    d. *World Book Encyclopedia*
    e. Gallup polls

14. Professor Dealy performed a historical analysis of race relations over the last 100 years and is now at work sorting out the findings, developing his opinions, and imposing some order on the findings by offering interpretations of the patterns detected. This analytical process is known as
    a. hermeneutics
    b. ideal type formation
    c. verstehen
    d. sociological historical analysis
    e. paradigm development

15. The basic difference between the historian and the sociologist in historical analysis is that the sociologist
    a. studies events more intensively
    b. interrelates specific events
    c. focuses on generalized understanding
    d. is less concerned with people and more with ideas
    e. uses numbers

DISCUSSION QUESTIONS

1. Compare and contrast content analysis, analysis of existing statistics, and historical/comparative analysis in terms of purposes, strengths, and weaknesses.

2. Explain why units of analysis are of particular concern in content analysis.

3. Explain why social science researchers are interested in both manifest and latent content. Show how they are both similar and different.

4. Discuss the special problems regarding validity and reliability experienced by those who analyze existing statistics.

EXERCISE 12.1

You are to compare three national news magazines in their coverage of some major news story in the past year.

1. First, select a news story that permitted different points of view. Note the story here.

2. Next, select three news magazines, from among such publications as *Newsweek, Time, U.S. News and World Reports, The New Republic, The Nation, National Review,* etc. (Your instructor may suggest others.) Pick three different issues of each magazine. Indicate the magazines and the dates of the issues you studied.

   Magazine 1 _____
      Date of first issue studied: _____
      Date of second issue studied: _____
      Date of third issue studied: _____

   Magazine 2 _____
      Date of first issue studied: _____
      Date of second issue studied: _____
      Date of third issue studied: _____

   Magazine 3 _____
      Date of first issue studied: _____
      Date of second issue studied: _____
      Date of third issue studied: _____

3. Describe the method you used to determine the relative amount of coverage each magazine devoted to the issue you are studying.

4. Report your findings regarding the amount of coverage each magazine devoted to the issue. Provide both data tabulations and your interpretations of those data.

5. Describe the method you used to determine the editorial positions taken by the magazines.

6. Report your findings regarding the editorial positions taken by the three magazines. Provide both data tabulations and your interpretations of those data.

EXERCISE 12.2

This exercise involves both content analysis and historical/comparative analysis. You are to do a content analysis of cartoons at three points in time.

1. First, select a magazine that has been in existence for at least 15 years. Pick three issues that are at least five years apart. Indicate the magazine and the dates of the issues you studied.

   Magazine _____
       Date of first issue studied: _____
       Date of second issue studied: _____
       Date of third issue studied: _____

2. Select cartoons that reflect a topic of interest to you, such as sex roles, the roles of older people, parent-child interactions, or power. Select three cartoons per issue of the magazine. Note the topic and attach the nine cartoons. Write the magazine title and date on each cartoon.

   Topic:

3. Describe the sampling methods you employed, if any.

4. Describe how you assessed manifest content.

195

5. Describe how you assessed latent content.

6. Report your findings, both quantitatively and nonquantitatively.

7. Interpret your results, paying particular attention to changes over time.

EXERCISE 12.3

Test the following hypothesis: States with large populations have higher auto theft rates than do states with small populations.

To test this hypothesis, you must determine the populations of each of the 50 states in some recent year and the number of auto thefts reported in each state that year. You might want to check the *Statistical Abstract of the United States*.

Complete the worksheet below, and rank order the 50 states in terms of population. Combine them into five groups of ten each, ranging from the ten smallest to the ten largest. Once you have them in groups of ten, combine the population for each group, combine the total number of thefts for each group, and divide the combined number of thefts by the combined population to get the auto theft rate for each group (see step 3).

1. Give the bibliographical citation of the source(s) from which your data are taken.

2. Complete the following worksheet:

	POPU-LATION	AUTO THEFTS		POPU-LATION	AUTO THEFTS
Alabama	____	____	Connecticut	____	____
Alaska	____	____	Delaware	____	____
Arizona	____	____	Florida	____	____
Arkansas	____	____	Georgia	____	____
California	____	____	Hawaii	____	____
Colorado	____	____	Idaho	____	____

Illinois	——	——	New York	——	——
Indiana	——	——	North Carolina	——	——
Iowa	——	——	North Dakota	——	——
Kansas	——	——	Ohio	——	——
Kentucky	——	——	Oklahoma	——	——
Louisiana	——	——	Oregon	——	——
Maine	——	——	Pennsylvania	——	——
Maryland	——	——	Rhode Island	——	——
Massachusetts	——	——	South Carolina	——	——
Michigan	——	——	South Dakota	——	——
Minnesota	——	——	Tennessee	——	——
Mississippi	——	——	Texas	——	——
Missouri	——	——	Utah	——	——
Montana	——	——	Vermont	——	——
Nebraska	——	——	Virginia	——	——
Nevada	——	——	Washington	——	——
New Hampshire	——	——	West Virginia	——	——
New Jersey	——	——	Wisconsin	——	——
New Mexico	——	——	Wyoming	——	——

3. Complete the following table (warning: be sure to convert states' auto theft *rates* into *numbers* of auto thefts before combining state figures):

	COMBINED POPULATION	COMBINED NUMBER OF AUTO THEFTS	COMBINED AUTO THEFT RATE
Smallest ten states	_____	_____	_____
Second smallest ten states	_____	_____	_____
Third smallest ten states	_____	_____	_____
Fourth smallest ten states	_____	_____	_____
Largest ten states	_____	_____	_____

4. Give a brief research report, indicating whether you feel the hypothesis was confirmed or disconfirmed.

Chapter 13

Evaluation Research

OBJECTIVES

1. Identify the purposes of evaluation research.

2. Identify three factors influencing the growth of evaluation research.

3. Define and illustrate social intervention.

4. Describe why it is important to identify the purpose of an intervention.

5. Define and illustrate the outcome (or response) variable.

6. Give three examples of experimental contexts that may influence specific evaluation research studies.

7. Describe two problems with specifying interventions.

8. Note the importance of specifying other variables, and give three specific examples of such variables.

9. Compare the two options for measuring variables.

10. Apply the classical experimental design to an evaluation research study.

11. Define quasi-experimental designs.

12. Define and illustrate time-series designs.

13. Define and illustrate nonequivalent control groups designs.

14. Define and illustrate multiple time-series designs.

15. Define and illustrate cost-benefit analysis.

16. Discuss why evaluation research is particularly subject to problems in the actual execution of the research.

17. Summarize three reasons why the implications of evaluation research are not always put into practice.

18. Define and illustrate social indicators research.

19. Define and illustrate computer simulation.

SUMMARY

Evaluation research employs the same research methods described in previous chapters. Its uniqueness lies in its purpose: to evaluate the impact of social interventions. It has experienced increased popularity due to the desire of social scientists to influence the quality of life as well as to increased federal requirements for program evaluation and the availability of research funds to meet those requirements.

Several topics are addressed with evaluation research. Critically important is a clear specification of both the purpose of the intervention to be evaluated as well as the measurement of the key variables. Researchers commonly specify different aspects of desired outcomes and allow for varying levels of success in meeting program objectives. The context within which the study occurs is critical, and hence these variables must be identified and measured as well. Extraneous variables must also be considered. Evaluation researchers must carefully identify the population of possible subjects for the study and must decide whether to create new measures or use existing measures. Measurement decisions are complicated by both practical and political considerations because evaluation researchers must work with the people responsible for the program that is being evaluated.

Some evaluation research studies employ the classical experimental design, in which subjects are randomly assigned to experimental and control groups. However, most evaluation research studies cannot meet the demands of random assignment and hence employ quasi-experimental designs. Time-series designs examine processes occurring over time. Nonequivalent control groups designs are used when an existing "control" group appears similar to the experimental group. Multiple time-series designs are an improved version of the nonequivalent control groups design and employ more than one time-series analysis.

Perhaps the most critical aspect of evaluation research is determining whether the program being studied succeeded or failed. Researchers typically allow for gradations of success or failure and frequently employ cost-benefit analysis to determine benefits relative to costs. But researchers find it difficult to assign exact dollar values.

In comparison to the traditional designs, evaluation research is prone to several types of problems. Logistical problems emerge because evaluation researchers often lack sufficient control over the design in real-life contexts. Researchers must also deal with reluctant and counterproductive administrators who wish to protect favorite programs. Social interventions frequently raise ethical issues, particularly regarding who receives and does not receive what type of stimulus.

Evaluation research is designed to be used to make a difference in the execution of some program. Results of evaluation research studies frequently contradict popular beliefs or personal beliefs of administrators involved. Evaluation researchers themselves often fail to present the implications of their research in a way that nonresearchers can understand. Sometimes, however, implications of evaluation studies are taken seriously, as demonstrated by the Manhattan Bail Bond project.

The use of social indicators has increased in recent years as a nonexperimental form of evaluation research. The use of such indicators makes it possible to monitor many aspects of social life on a large scale. With computer simulation, evaluation researchers can develop mathematical equations describing the relationships that link social variables to one another. By varying one or more of the variables in the equation, social scientists can examine the implications of specific changes.

TERMS

1. applied research
2. computer simulation
3. evaluation research
4. experimental contexts
5. multiple time-series designs
6. nonequivalent control groups designs
7. outcome/response variable
8. quasi-experimental designs
9. social intervention
10. social indicators
11. time-series designs
12. vested interests

MATCHING

____ 1. The general class of experimental designs that lack random assignment subjects to experimental and control groups.

____ 2. The variable that reflects the result of an intervention.

____ 3. A type of quasi-experimental design that uses a comparison group rather than a control group to which subjects are randomly assigned.

____ 4. Aspects of societies that are monitored.

____ 5. Ego involvement in a project that often hampers the implementation of evaluation research results.

____ 6. A form of applied research that assesses the impact of social interventions.

____ 7. The general class of research that is intended to have some real-world effect.

____ 8. Variables external to the experiment itself, yet affecting it.

REVIEW QUESTIONS

1. Evaluation research employs which method(s)?
   a. surveys

b. experiments
c. observation
d. existing statistics
e. all of the above

2. Which one of the following is **correct?**
   a. evaluation research is a form of program evaluation
   b. evaluation research is a form of applied research
   c. applied research is a form of evaluation research
   d. applied research is a form of program evaluation
   e. program evaluation is a form of survey research

3. The recent growth of evaluation research is due primarily to
   a. increased methodological sophistication
   b. the spurt in the number of social scientists
   c. increased federal requirements and financial support
   d. disagreement over policy implications
   e. the decline in quality of services rendered by social service agencies

4. Which one of the following is an example of a social intervention?
   a. a study of dating behavior among college students
   b. a study of the effect of sex on participation in voluntary associations
   c. a study of the effect of religiosity on income
   d. a study of the effect of team teaching on learning
   e. a study of the effect of organizational size on productivity

5. The **most** critical problem in evaluation research is
   a. dealing with ethical issues
   b. measuring the outcome
   c. developing an adequate sample
   d. dealing with political constraints
   e. developing appropriate statistical techniques

6. The **key** issue in specifying and measuring outcomes is
   a. to consider multiple outcomes and multiple indicators of each
   b. to rank order the outcomes
   c. to reflect the importance attached to outcomes by program administrators
   d. to consult clients
   e. to employ scaling techniques

7. Which of the following strategies is particularly useful for measuring the effects of experimental contexts?
    a. multiple regression
    b. multiple indicators
    c. involving clients
    d. blind designs
    e. control groups

8. Measures that have been used previously are likely to have higher degrees of
    a. conceptual diversity
    b. dimensionality
    c. validity and reliability
    d. statistical rigor
    e. datedness

9. Quasi-experimental designs differ from "true" experimental designs
    a. by shorter duration and more political constraints
    b. by more political constraints and more ethical considerations
    c. by more ethical considerations and lack of random assignment
    d. by lack of random assignment and lack of a control group
    e. by lack of a control group and shorter duration

10. Professor Gabino wants to do an evaluation research study on the effect of a new treatment for learning disabilities. She has only one group of clients and wants to assess the effects over the course of a couple of months. Which design would be best?
    a. classical
    b. nonequivalent control group
    c. time-series
    d. posttest-only control group design
    e. factorial

11. Professor Yee wants to do an evaluation study of the effects of a patient education program on patient anxiety. He uses one wing in a hospital for the experiment and compares the results with a similar group of patients in a similar wing in another hospital. Which design would be best?
    a. classical
    b. nonequivalent control group
    c. time-series

d. posttest-only control group design
e. factorial

12. Cost-benefit analysis is used to assess
    a. the long-term effect on clients
    b. the cost of the experiment relative to the social scientific knowledge gained
    c. how much of an increase of effect is sufficient for success, given cost
    d. the costs to society relative to the benefits to the clients
    e. the costs of the program relative to the number of staff hours invested

13. Evaluation researchers encounter more logistical problems than other researchers because evaluation research
    a. occurs in the context of real life
    b. takes longer
    c. is more costly
    d. has more measurement problems
    e. examines more variables

14. The ethical issues of evaluation research center on
    a. the policy implications
    b. the administrators of the agency
    c. the nature of the clients
    d. the nature of the social intervention
    e. informed consent

15. Computer simulation is particularly useful for
    a. measuring social indicators
    b. analyzing many variables
    c. outlining policy implications
    d. improving reliability and validity
    e. predicting outcomes of specific social changes

DISCUSSION QUESTIONS

1. Discuss why measurement is important in evaluation research. Describe the role of measurement in each of the four types of variables Babbie discusses.

2. Explain why evaluation researchers find it difficult to employ the classical experimental design, which is best suited to establishing causality. Which designs are more typically used? Why?

3. What are the major reasons why evaluation research results are often ignored? What could be done to remedy this situation?

4. Discuss some of the ethical problems that are particularly troublesome in doing evaluation research.

5. Economists have developed a substantial number of indicators to monitor the country's economic health (consumer price index, unemployment rate, and others), many of which are a part of the daily news. How would you explain the scarcity of noneconomic social indicators in the coverage of social issues?

EXERCISE 13.1

The purpose of this workbook is to give you some firsthand experience in applying the various aspects of social research, on the assumption that you will learn research methods better that way. The purpose of this workbook, then, is to assist you in understanding the various aspects of social research. In this exercise, you are to design an evaluation study to determine the effectiveness of this workbook. You are planning your project now for implementation next year. So you have some control over the setting in creating your design.

Describe all aspects of your study design, including the likely conclusions.

1. Give specific information regarding the following types of variables: outcomes, experimental contexts, intervention, and other variables. How will you measure each?

2. Describe which design you selected and why. Outline the study in detail in terms of this design.

3. Describe possible logistical and ethical problems and how you would handle them.

4. Present some fake data and interpret the results.

EXERCISE 13.2

You are to design an evaluation research study. Look through your local newspaper and find a report of some innovative social program, such as prison reform, a program to provide jobs to young people during school vacations, or a proposal for a new welfare system. Or simply select an innovative social program you are interested in. Describe how you would evaluate the success of the program.

1. Briefly describe the innovative program.

2. Specify the key dependent variable that is influenced by the program.

3. Describe as specifically as possible how you would measure that dependent variable.

4. How would you design and conduct your evaluation of the program? Be sure to describe any ways in which the program itself would have to be modified in order to permit your evaluation. Also, specify the data you would need to collect.

5. Write a hypothetical research report, reporting the "results" of your evaluation of the program. Make up data, and be sure to give your conclusion about the program's success or failure, along with reasons for this conclusion.

EXERCISE 13.3

You have been asked to develop a composite measure of the quality of life on your campus.

1. Outline the social indicators you would use to develop such a measure. Be specific. Explain why you selected these indicators.

2. Now suppose data on your social indicators have been collected over a ten-year period. What might you be able to do with these data?

Part 4

Analysis of Data

Chapter 14

Quantifying Data

OBJECTIVES

1. Define machine-readable form.

2. Define field.

3. Describe an IBM card.

4. Define precoding.

5. Describe the logical function of the counter-sorter.

6. Describe the functions of the computer.

7. Define remote job entry.

8. Define time sharing and describe its use for social science data analysis.

9. Illustrate the use of computer network.

10. Note the utility of microcomputers.

11. Describe the coding process and compare two approaches to developing code categories.

12. Summarize the various data entry options: transfer sheets, edge-coding, direct data entry, data entry by interviewers, and direct use of optical scan sheets.

13. Illustrate the use of a codebook.

14. Explain the purpose of data cleaning.

15. Compare possible-code cleaning and contingency cleaning.

16. Give two examples of possible-code cleaning and two examples of contingency cleaning.

SUMMARY

This chapter describes methods of converting social science data into machine-readable form, which can be read and manipulated by computers. This area is experiencing rapid expansion, although most technologies follow the basic card format.

An IBM card (or its equivalent) contains 80 vertical columns, each containing ten spaces. Data are stored on cards by punching holes in the columns with the keypunch machine or by inputting the data on a terminal. Each variable is assigned a field of one or more columns on the card; the number punched in a field corresponds to an attribute of a variable. Each card (or its video equivalent) represents a single unit of analysis, and each column (or set of columns) stores the same variable on each card.

Punched data cards used to be read by counter-sorters and by cardreaders linked to computers, but now they are input directly via terminals. The counter-sorter sorts a deck of cards into slots corresponding to the punches for a given column; counters on the machine tabulate cards sorted into each slot. The computer avoids the limitations of the counter-sorter by not being limited to the physical manipulation of cards and by being able to perform detailed analyses. Unlike the counter-sorter, the computer can analyze multiple cards per unit of analysis and can read disks and tapes. Social scientists typically use a computer package, which eliminates many programming responsibilities.

Computer usage continues to become easier and more efficient. Remote job entry systems make it easy for a researcher to submit and retrieve computer submissions from his or her office. Time-sharing enables mainframe computers to perform many tasks simultaneously. Terminals can be linked with nationwide computer networks, which allow access to many data sets and analysis programs (in addition to many other options). Microcomputers are self-contained and perform many of the functions of mainframe computers. They also can be linked to mainframe computers and used as terminals.

Data must be converted to numerical codes in order to perform quantitative analysis. Code numbers must be assigned either as part of the observation process (as in content analysis) or after the data have been collected. The task of coding involves specifying an appropriate number of attributes for a given variable. The coding scheme may already be established before the data are examined, or it may be developed after examining a number of cases to determine what set of code categories would be most appropriate.

A codebook is a document that describes the locations of variables and lists the codes assigned to the attributes of the variables. It is the primary guide used in the coding process and serves as a guide for locating variables and interpreting the attributes of variables. The codebook also helps the researcher to decide which variables should be examined in which fashion.

There are several methods by which coding and data entry can be integrated. Although seldom done, coded data can be recorded onto transfer sheets, which are special forms ruled off in 80 columns (like a data card), with each row representing an individual card. The key-puncher then punches the data from transfer sheets onto cards or enters the data into a terminal. This "punching" may then be verified. Edge-coding involves recording code numbers in the margins of questionnaires or other data-source documents. Adequately precoded questionnaires make it possible to enter data directly from completed questionnaires, thereby eliminating the need for transfer sheets or edge-coding. Another method involves inputting data directly from questionnaires. With interviews, responses can be typed directly into a computer. Optical scan sheets, marked either by coders or by respondents, can sometimes be used to facilitate data entry.

Once data entry has occurred and the data have been verified, the resulting set of data should be checked for errors and the errors corrected. Possible-code cleaning involves checking each variable for invalid entries—code numbers that are not supposed to occur. Computerized data entry systems automatically check for such irregularities. Contingency cleaning is a more complicated procedure used to check for the joint occurrence of codes that could not logically go together.

TERMS

1. acoustical coupler
2. codebook
3. coding
4. computer networks
5. contingency cleaning
6. direct data entry
7. edge-coding
8. field
9. microcomputer
10. optical scanner
11. possible-code cleaning
12. remote job entry
13. time-sharing
14. transfer sheet

MATCHING

_____ 1. A data entry option that uses the outside margin of a questionnaire.

_____ 2. A data entry option that involves keying in responses directly on a video screen.

_____ 3. A document that describes the locations of variables and lists the code assignments to the attributes of those variables.

_____ 4. Specific columns of a data card assigned to a variable.

_____ 5. The process by which a coder eliminates inappropriate codes by comparing codes with a list of correct values.

_____ 6. Small self-contained computers.

_____ 7. An arrangement whereby computers process many jobs at the same time.

_____ 8. An arrangement whereby data entry machines and printers are not near the mainframe computer.

REVIEW QUESTIONS

1. The end product of quantifying data is to convert measurements into
   a. scales
   b. typologies
   c. machine-readable forms
   d. counter-sorter forms
   e. bytes

2. An IBM card (or its video equivalent) has how many columns?
   a. 20
   b. 40
   c. 60
   d. 80
   e. 100

3. Columns 18-23 contain data for respondents' income. This group of columns is known as a
   a. record length
   b. field
   c. byte
   d. case
   e. deck

4. The counter-sorter was used primarily to
   a. improve reliability
   b. construct contingency tables
   c. group together all the cards for a given respondent
   d. perform sophisticated statistical analyses
   e. restructure record length

5. The history of computing began with
   a. IBM
   b. Census Bureau employee Hollerith
   c. the Chinese
   d. a French textile worker
   e. the Japanese

6. Professor Dawson wants the computer to show the coder which items to code to improve coders' accuracy. Which data entry method would be best?

a. direct use of optical scan sheets
b. coding to optical scan sheets
c. transfer sheets
d. edge-coding
e. direct data entry

7. Professor Lowry will do a questionnaire study of 300 seniors in her class. All the questions are closed-ended with no more than five answers. Which of the following would be the *best* strategy to perform coding and data entry?
a. transfer sheets
b. edge-coding
c. direct punching
d. direct use of optical scan sheet
e. coding to optical scan sheets

8. After coding and data entry but before data analysis, data must be
a. sorted by case
b. repunched
c. cleaned
d. sorted by field
e. massaged

9. Pat wanted to check the accuracy of her data entry procedures and did so by checking for logical inconsistencies among the responses to several items. For example, she would recheck the original data if someone was coded as unemployed but was coded on another variable as working 37 hours last week. Which method did she use?
a. possible-code cleaning
b. direct data entry
c. optical scan cleaning
d. remote data cleaning
e. contingency cleaning

10. George used his portable computer to link with the mainframe computer at school. He ran a few jobs that the computer processed simultaneously with several dozen other jobs, and he communicated with his professor via a network. This situation reflects
a. the future
b. time-sharing
c. indirect data entry and retrieval

d.   a misuse of computer
e.   direct data entry and retrieval

DISCUSSION QUESTIONS

1. Summarize the history of computers.

2. Describe the role of microcomputers in social research.

3. Describe and compare the following data entry options: transfer sheets, edge-coding, coding to optical scan sheets, direct use of optical scan sheets, and direct data entry. Discuss the possible sources of error in using each approach.

4. Describe and compare the two types of data cleaning strategies: possible-code cleaning and contingency cleaning. Which is better? Why?

EXERCISE 14.1

The following page contains a copy of the questionnaire used in Exercise 10.2. For each variable, describe the item or variable number and name, the meaning (answer category) for each number associated with each attribute of the variable, and the column number you assigned to the variable. Include column numbers for the case ID and sex.

Variable Number	Variable Name	Response Codes and Meanings	Column Number

Case ID_____   Respondent's sex: [ ] Male [ ] Female

Hello. My name is _____ and I'm conducting a short survey as part of an exercise for my research methods class. Would you be willing to participate in the study? The interview will take less than five minutes. (ENCOURAGE IF RELUCTANT.)

I'm going to read some opinions about the effects of looking at or reading sexual materials. As I read each one, please tell me if you think sexual materials do or do not have that effect. (READ EACH ITEM AND CHECK THE APPROPRIATE CATEGORY.)

	Yes	No	Don't Know	No Answer
1. Sexual materials provide information about sex.	[ ]	[ ]	[ ]	[ ]
2. Sexual materials lead to a breakdown of morals.	[ ]	[ ]	[ ]	[ ]
3. Sexual materials lead people to commit rape.	[ ]	[ ]	[ ]	[ ]
4. Sexual materials provide an outlet for bottled-up impulses.	[ ]	[ ]	[ ]	[ ]

I am going to name some institutions in this country. As far as the PEOPLE RUNNING these institutions are concerned, would you say that you have a great deal of confidence, only some confidence, or hardly any confidence at all in them? (CODE FOR EACH ITEM; CODE DK FOR "DON'T KNOW" OR NA FOR "NO ANSWER" IF APPROPRIATE.)

	Great Deal	Only Some	Hardly Any	DK	NA
5. Education	[ ]	[ ]	[ ]	[ ]	[ ]
6. Press	[ ]	[ ]	[ ]	[ ]	[ ]
7. Congress	[ ]	[ ]	[ ]	[ ]	[ ]

8. Could you tell me, in your own words, how you feel about the "Women's Liberation Movement"?

That completes the interview. Thank you for your cooperation.

EXERCISE 14.2

You are to code the responses you got in answer to Question 8 of the questionnaire used in Exercise 10.2.

Code each of the responses as:

(1) favorable to the Women's Liberation Movement

(2) unfavorable to the Women's Liberation Movement

(3) neutral to the Women's Liberation Movement

	RESPONSE	CODE (1,2,3)
1.	_____	_____
2.	_____	_____
3.	_____	_____
4.	_____	_____
5.	_____	_____
6.	_____	_____
7.	_____	_____
8.	_____	_____
9.	_____	_____
10.	_____	_____

EXERCISE 14.3

An abbreviated transfer sheet is provided below. Enter the data gathered in the 10 interviews conducted in Exercise 10.2 and coded in Exercises 14.1 and 14.2. Use the codesheet prepared in the previous exercise as a guide for the location of your data.

Case #	\multicolumn{12}{c}{Columns}
	1	2	3	4	5	6	7	8	9	10	11	12
1												
2												
3												
4												
5												
6												
7												
8												
9												
10												

EXERCISE 14.4

1. Prepare these data for input to the computers on your campus. Your instructor will provide details.

2. Verify the data after completing step 1.

Chapter 15

Elementary Analyses

OBJECTIVES

1. Describe a contingency table.

2. Define and give examples of univariate analysis.

3. Define and explain the utility of frequency distributions and marginals.

4. Explain how to calculate percentages.

5. Define central tendency.

6. Compare the mode, mean, and median in terms of calculation and interpretation.

7. Describe the information provided by measures of dispersion.

8. Compare the range, standard deviation, and interquartile range in terms of calculation and interpretation.

9. Distinguish continuous variables from discrete variables by definition and example.

10. Provide guidelines for balancing the demands of detail versus manageability of data presentation.

11. Differentiate the goals of univariate, bivariate, and multivariate analyses.

12. Identify the goal of subgroup comparisons.

13. Explain two techniques for handling the "don't know" response.

14. Differentiate dependent variable from independent variable by definition and example.

15. Describe how bivariate tables are presented and analyzed.

16. Explain how multivariate tables are presented and analyzed.

SUMMARY

Social scientists perform a variety of analysis strategies on their data. There are three basic strategies: univariate analysis, bivariate analysis, and multivariate analysis.

Univariate analysis involves the examination of only one variable at a time. Data are organized into frequency distributions, which are listings of the number of cases in each attribute of a variable. Each case may be listed separately, or they may be grouped in the form of marginals. Marginals sacrifice some detail in the data but provide a more manageable format for describing a distribution. In addition to raw numbers, percentages may be presented by dividing the number of cases per attribute by the base. Careful attention must be paid to determining the base, particularly in the case of missing data.

The detailed information in raw data may be simplified by calculating a measure of central tendency, a single value that summarizes a distribution. The mode reflects the attribute with the greatest frequency; the mean is calculated by summing the values and dividing by the number of cases; and the median reflects the value that cuts the distribution in half.

Because measures of central tendency fail to indicate the spread of scores in a distribution, measures of dispersion are calculated to reflect this spread of scores. The range is the distance between the highest and lowest values; the standard deviation reflects the difference between each score and the mean; and the interquartile range reflects the range after removing the top fourth and bottom fourth of the scores.

Which measure of dispersion or central tendency to use is determined by the nature of the data and the purpose of the analysis. For example, continuous variables and discrete variables are treated differently. Researchers sometimes violate some of the statistical assumptions, and this is legitimate to the extent that it helps interpret the data. But be aware that such procedures may lead you to think that the results represent something truly precise. Researchers are also constrained by the conflicting goals of providing complete detail versus presenting data in a manageable format.

Subgroup comparisons yield a descriptive analysis to two variables by presenting descriptive univariate data for each of several subgroups. Occasionally categories must be collapsed to enhance the analysis. "Don't know" responses can be included or excluded, depending on the purpose of the study. Subgroup comparisons focus on describing the people (or other units of analysis), and bivariate analysis focuses on the relationship between the variables themselves. Hence bivariate analysis assumes an explanatory goal.

The explanatory goal of bivariate analysis involves making causal assertions regarding a dependent variable that is at least partially determined by an independent variable. Hence bivariate analysis tables should be consistent with the logic of independent and dependent variables. Typically the attributes of the independent variable are used as column headings, and the attributes of the dependent variables are used as row headings. Percentages are then computed down (adding up to 100 percent) and compared across. But these conventions are sometimes reversed. Regardless of how a bivariate analysis is presented, it is critical to interpret such a table by comparing the independent variable subgroups with one another in terms of the attributes of the dependent variable.

Several guidelines should be followed in presenting and interpreting contingency tables: (1) the contents of the table should be described in a title; (2) the original content of the variables should be clearly presented in either the table itself or the text; (3) the attributes of each variable should be clearly described; (4) the base on which percentages are computed should be shown; and (5) the table should indicate the number of cases omitted from the analysis.

The logic and procedures in bivariate tabular analysis also apply to multivariate tables. But instead of explaining a dependent variable on the basis of one independent variable, such analysis explains a dependent variable on the basis of multiple independent variables. Both the separate and the combined effects of the independent variables on the dependent variable can then be examined. When the dependent variable is dichotomous, the multivariate table can be simplified by omitting the data for one attribute of the dependent variable. The two independent variables are then typically placed on the top and the side of a table, and the percentages recorded reflect one attribute of the dependent variable for each combination of attributes of the independent variables. The base for each cell should be reported.

TERMS

1. base
2. bivariate analysis
3. central tendency
4. contingency table
5. continuous variable
6. dependent variable
7. discrete variable
8. dispersion
9. frequency distribution
10. independent variable
11. interquartile range
12. marginals
13. mean
14. median
15. mode
16. multivariate analysis
17. percentages
18. range
19. standard deviation
20. subgroup comparisons
21. univariate analysis

MATCHING

____ 1. The examination of the effects of two or more independent variables on a dependent variable.

____ 2. A measure of central tendency that measures the most frequent attribute.

____ 3. The measure of central tendency that is the arithmetic average.

____ 4. The measure of central tendency that divides the distribution in half.

____ 5. The measure of dispersion that resembles the standard error of a sampling distribution and that is interpreted in terms of the normal curve.

___ 6. A method of univariate analysis that simply reports the number of cases in each attribute category.

___ 7. A variable that influences another variable.

___ 8. A variable that is influenced by another variable.

REVIEW QUESTIONS

1. Which one of the following is an example of a frequency distribution of grouped data for age?
   a. 18-25, 40 people; 26-50, 60 people; over 50, 20 people
   b. 18, 10 people; 19, 11 people; 20, 26 people; 21, 15 people
   c. 26, 28, 28, 30, 31, 33, 35, 41, 41, 50
   d. the mean age is 45.1
   e. the median age is 38.6

2. Frequency distributions of grouped data are often referred to as
   a. indexicals
   b. dispersion
   c. epsilon
   d. monotonicity
   e. marginals

3. The *most* critical issue in calculating percentages in univariate analysis is
   a. making sure enough cases exist in each category
   b. determining the appropriate base
   c. deciding whether to percentage down or across
   d. making sure they add up to 100 percent
   e. applying the correct formula

4. Which measure of central tendency divides the distribution into two halves?
   a. dispersion
   b. mode
   c. marginal
   d. median
   e. mean

5. With several extreme scores, which measure of dispersion would be most appropriate?
   a. range
   b. standard deviation
   c. standard error
   d. confidence level
   e. interquartile range

6. Regarding the calculation of means for ordinal level data and other violations of statistical assumptions, it is best to
   a. do it if it is useful in understanding the data
   b. do it only if the sample size is large enough
   c. do it if enough indicators are used
   d. not do it unless it is the only way to get some statistics
   e. never do it

7. A fundamental dilemma in presenting data is
   a. scope versus adequacy
   b. nominal versus ordinal values
   c. univariate versus bivariate
   d. detail versus manageability
   e. variation versus central tendency

8. Descriptive analyses are most often accomplished with which type of statistical analysis?
   a. bivariate
   b. univariate
   c. dispersion
   d. multivariate
   e. interpretation

9. Comparing the church attendance of men and women for descriptive purposes is an example of
   a. univariate analysis
   b. multivariate analysis
   c. subgroup comparisons
   d. explanatory analysis
   e. bivariate analysis

10. Professor Dorn analyzed the relationship between age and voting behavior. This is an example of which type of analysis?
    a. univariate
    b. bivariate
    c. multivariate
    d. descriptive
    e. ex post facto

11. The fundamental rule in reading tables is to
    a. percentage down
    b. percentage across
    c. read across the categories of the dependent variable in analyzing the independent variable
    d. read across along the categories of the independent variable in analyzing the dependent variable
    e. percentage and read in terms of the total number of cases

12. Another term for bivariate tables is
    a. dependency tables
    b. independency tables
    c. marginals tables
    d. cross-sectional tables
    e. contingency tables

13. Professor Goldsmid studied the relationship between sex and religiosity while controlling for social class. This is an example of which type of analysis?
    a. univariate
    b. bivariate
    c. multivariate analysis
    d. descriptive
    e. ex post facto

14. Combining two independent variables and one dependent variable into one table is possible *only* when
    a. the dependent variable is dichotomous
    b. the independent variables are dichotomous
    c. both the independent and dependent variables are dichotomous
    d. a test of statistical significance is applied
    e. a bivariate analysis is done

DISCUSSION QUESTIONS

1. Compare univariate and bivariate analyses in terms of definition, purpose, advantages, and limitations.

2. Compare the three measures of central tendency (mode, median, mean) in terms of definition, calculation, interpretation, and limitations.

3. Subgroup comparison is considered to be somewhat intermediate between univariate and bivariate analyses. In what sense does subgroup analysis serve a descriptive purpose, and in what sense does it serve an explanatory purpose?

4. Explain the logic in constructing and interpreting bivariate tables. Why should you percentage within categories of the independent variable and then compare across categories?

EXERCISE 15.1

The number of movies attended in the preceding three months are given below for 30 people. Calculate the mean, the median, the mode, and the range. Show your work. Interpret each statistic.

0	15	26	8	2
3	11	13	0	3
0	1	17	1	9
7	4	18	12	10
10	4	2	7	2
2	5	9	6	6

1. Calculate the mean and interpret the results.

2. Calculate the median and interpret the results.

3. Calculate the mode and interpret the results.

4. Compare the three measures of central tendency you have calculated in terms of the information provided.

5. Calculate the range and interpret the results.

EXERCISE 15.2

Presented below are some hypothetical data representing 50 people: (1) sex (M=male, F=female) and (2) whether they attended church last week (Y=yes, N=no).

In the steps below you will be asked to construct the appropriate bivariate percentage table showing the relationship between sex and church attendance and to give your interpretation of that table.

M-N	F-N	F-Y	M-N	M-Y	F-N	F-Y	F-Y	M-N	M-Y
M-Y	F-Y	M-N	M-Y	F-Y	F-N	M-N	M-N	F-N	F-Y
M-N	F-Y	M-N	M-Y	F-Y	F-Y	M-N	M-N	F-Y	M-N
F-Y	M-N	M-Y	F-Y	F-N	F-Y	M-Y	F-Y	M-N	M-N
F-Y	F-Y	M-N	F-N	M-N	F-Y	M-N	F-Y	F-Y	M-N

1. Construct the bivariate percentage table appropriate for examining the relationship between sex and church attendance.

2. Give your interpretation of the table you have constructed.

EXERCISE 15.3

Select about eight variables that interest you from the General Social Survey codebook in Appendix 1 of this workbook. If you also plan to do Exercise 15.4, make sure that about half can be considered independent variables and that about half can be considered dependent variables. Produce a frequency distribution of the variables, using SPSS^x (see Appendix H in the text). Your program should resemble the following:

```
FREQUENCIES  VARIABLES=VAR1, VAR2, VAR3, etc./
    FORMAT ONEPAGE/
    HISTOGRAM/
    STATISTICS=DEFAULT MEDIAN MODE RANGE
```

Use your variable names in place of the VAR1, etc. in the program above. A histogram will be produced, and the program card will produce the mean, standard deviation, minimum, maximum, median, mode, and range.

Interpret both the frequency distributions and the appropriate statistics for five of the variables. Your interpretations should mention the level of measurement of each variable and refer only to those statistics appropriate for that level. (Note that the computer will calculate any statistics on your data whether appropriate or not.) Write your interpretations directly on the output (unless your instructor advises otherwise). Finally, write your name on the top page and list the page numbers containing your analyses.

EXERCISE 15.4

Construct six tables from the variables you analyzed in Exercise 15.3 involving the General Social Survey codebook contained in Appendix 1 of this workbook (or select sufficient independent and dependent variables now if you have not done Exercise 15.3). Use SPSS^x (see Appendix H in the text) to produce the tables. Remember to list your dependent variables before the "BY" and the independent variables after the "BY." Your program should resemble the following:

```
CROSSTABS   TABLES=VAR1 VAR2 VAR3 BY VAR4 VAR5
OPTIONS     4,9
STATISTICS  ALL (or as noted by your instructor)
```

Use your variable names in place of the VAR1, etc. in the program above. The OPTIONS instruction will make the tables easier to read by printing only the within column percentages and will produce an index of all the tables. The STATISTICS instruction will produce chi square as well as various measures of association.

Select two tables to interpret. Be sure to (1) compare percentages, (2) summarize the relationship, and (3) briefly explain the relationship. (Your task of learning how to read the tables might be more meaningful at this point if you choose variables with relatively few categories. This simplifies the structure of the tables.) Do this directly on the output (unless your instructor advises otherwise). Write your name on the top page and list the page numbers containing your analyses.

Ignore the statistics for now; they will be used in a later exercise.

EXERCISE 15.5

Presented below is a hypothetical trivariate percentage table.

	Percentage in Favor of the Women's Liberation Movement	
	Men	Women
Young	60%	80%
Old	20%	25%

1. Explain the logical structure of the table.

2. Give your interpretation of the table.

Chapter 16

The Elaboration Model

OBJECTIVES

1. Describe the goal of the elaboration model.

2. Summarize the historical origins of the elaboration model.

3. Define and illustrate control variables.

4. Define partial tables and partial relationships.

5. Differentiate antecedent from intervening variables by definition and example.

6. Differentiate the following outcomes of the elaboration model by definition and example: replication, explanation, interpretation, and specification.

7. Differentiate a suppressor variable from a distorter variable by definition and example.

8. Discuss the positive and negative features of ex post facto hypothesizing.

SUMMARY

The elaboration model involves multivariate analysis to portray more clearly the relationship between two variables by introducing additional control variables. The elaboration model derives historically from Samuel Stouffer's research during World War II. Faced with unexpected findings from studies of soldier morale, Stouffer suggested logical explanations for the findings based on the theoretical concepts of reference group and deprivation. Patricia Kendall and Paul Lazarsfeld later formalized the elaboration model suggested in Stouffer's work by constructing hypothetical tables consistent with Stouffer's explanations.

The elaboration model extends a bivariate relationship by introducing a control variable. The entire sample is divided into the categories of the control variable, and then the original bivariate relationship for each subgroup is recomputed separately. The resulting partial relationships, one for each attribute of the control variable, are then compared with the original bivariate relationship to determine the effect of the control variable on the original relationship.

There are four major outcomes possible in elaboration analysis. Replication occurs whenever the partial relationships are essentially the same as the original bivariate relationship. Hence the original relationship has been replicated under test conditions. Specification occurs when the partial relationships are significantly different from each other. For example, the original bivariate relationship may be found in one subgroup but not in the other. This outcome specifies the conditions under which the relationship occurs or fails to occur.

Before the next two outcomes can be identified, i.e., explanation and interpretation, the control variable must be identified as antecedent to the other two variables or as intervening between them. Explanation occurs when an original bivariate relationship is explained away through the introduction of a control variable, and the control variable is antecedent to both the independent and dependent variables. The partial relationships must be zero or significantly less than those found in the original relationship. Such an explained relationship is often called a spurious relationship. On the other hand, similar findings can be the result of interpretation when the control variable occurs between the independent and dependent variables rather than prior to both variables. The partial relationships must again be zero or significantly less than those found in the original relationship.

Methodologists have extended the elaboration model beyond that formulated by Stouffer and by Kendall and Lazarsfeld. For example, Rosenberg suggested using the elaboration model even when the original relationship is zero. Doing so may uncover a suppressor variable, which conceals the relationship in the original table. The basic model also fails to provide guidelines for specifying what constitutes a significant difference between the original and the partials and fails to consider the possibility that partial relationships might be stronger or the reverse of the original. The latter case is caused by a distorter variable. Finally, the basic approach employs only dichotomous control variables, but nondichotomous control variables can also be used.

Ex post facto hypothesizing occurs when a social scientist observes an empirical relationship and then suggests one or more hypotheses to explain that relationship. On the surface, this procedure violates the principle that hypotheses must be disconfirmable and is, therefore, inappropriate. But the elaboration model often provides the opportunity to suggest and test additional hypotheses regarding a bivariate relationship once the data are already at hand. The acceptance of hypotheses is primarily a function of the extent to which they have been tested by elaboration and not disconfirmed; ex post facto hypothesizing may be a central part of this testing process if it is appropriately applied.

TERMS

1. antecedent variable
2. control variable
3. distorter variable
4. elaboration model
5. explanation
6. ex post facto hypothesizing
7. interpretation

8. intervening variable
9. partial relationships
10. partial tables
11. replication
12. specification
13. spurious relationship
14. suppressor variable

MATCHING

_____ 1. The technique used to understand the relationship between two variables through the simultaneous introduction of additional variables.

_____ 2. A variable used to divide the sample into subsets so that the original relationship can be examined in each of the subsets.

_____ 3. A variable that comes before both the independent and dependent variables.

_____ 4. A variable that comes between the independent and dependent variables.

_____ 5. Occurs when the partial relationships are essentially the same as the original relationship.

_____ 6. Occurs when the original relationship can be explained in terms of an intervening variable.

_____ 7. Occurs when the original relationship can be explained in terms of an antecedent variable.

_____ 8. Occurs when partial relationships differ significantly from each other.

REVIEW QUESTIONS

1. The basis of the elaboration model is *best* summarized as follows
   a.   understanding the effects of antecedent variables
   b.   understanding the relationship between two variables through the controlled introduction of other variables
   c.   understanding the effects of intervening variables
   d.   explaining relationships between two variables that crop up inadvertently
   e.   supporting the findings of the partial relationships as compared with the original relationships

2. The *key* feature of the control variable that determines the type of elaboration is
   a.   the number of categories
   b.   if there are more than one
   c.   the number of partials
   d.   the time order
   e.   the strength of the relationship

3. Professor Kinkle conducted a survey in which he found that people over the age of 40 were more likely to put their parents in nursing homes than were people under age 40. When he controlled for age of parents, the results remained the same. This is an example of
   a.   replication
   b.   explanation
   c.   specification
   d.   interpretation
   e.   ex post facto hypothesizing

4. Researcher Lutter studied differences in men and women in degrees of stubbornness and found women to be more stubborn than men. When she controlled out for zodiac signs, she found that the relationship held only under the sign of Taurus. This is an example of
   a. replication
   b. explanation
   c. specification
   d. interpretation
   e. ex post facto hypothesizing

5. The type of elaboration analysis that lends credibility and validity to a finding at the bivariate level is
   a. replication
   b. specification
   c. explanation
   d. interpretation
   e. ex post facto hypothesizing

6. A. The original relationship between sex and voting:

	Male	Female
Voted	60%	50%
Did not vote	40%	50%
Total	100%	100%

B. The relationship between sex and voting, but *only* for those *under* 35:

	Male	Female
Voted	20%	70%
Did not vote	80%	30%
Total	100%	100%

C. The relationship between sex and voting, but *only* for those *over* 35:

	Male	Female
Voted	40%	50%
Did not vote	60%	50%
Total	100%	100%

Which type of elaboration is reflected in these tables?
a. replication
b. explanation
c. specification
d. interpretation
e. reductionism

7. In the tables in the preceding question, which is/are partial tables(s)?
   a. A
   b. B
   c. C
   d. all three
   e. B and C only

8. Professor Delphia found a relationship between sex and occupational status. When he controlled for SES, the relationship disappeared. This is an example of
   a. replication
   b. explanation
   c. specification
   d. interpretation
   e. ex post facto hypothesizing

9. In the above example "SES" is a/an
   a. independent variable
   b. antecedent variable
   c. intervening variable
   d. suppressor variable
   e. distorter variable

10. Professor Rodriquez found a strong positive relationship between participation in high school activities and occupational success. She then controlled for social class background and the relationship vanished. Which type of elaboration is reflected in this example?
    a. replication
    b. specification
    c. interpretation
    d. explanation
    e. ex post facto hypothesizing

11. A spurious relationship is most likely to be identified with which type of elaboration?
    a. replication
    b. explanation
    c. interpretation
    d. specification
    e. ex post facto hypothesizing

12. Which of the following is *not* a limitation to the basic elaboration paradigm?
    a. it assumes an initial relationship
    b. it does not specify what constitutes a significant difference between the original and partial relationships
    c. it ignores the fact that partials may be stronger than the original relationship
    d. it focuses primarily on dichotomous variables
    e. all are limitations

13. Professor Luan is conducting research on the relationship between the number of hours a student studies and the grade received on a test. Inadvertently she discovers that the number of pizzas consumed the previous day is related to test performance. She concludes that students who take time out for themselves to relax are more likely to get higher grades than those who do not. This is an example of
    a. replication
    b. explanation
    c. specification
    d. interpretation
    e. ex post facto hypothesizing

14. Originally, when Professor Elizabeth examined the relationship between the number of mice in an apartment and the emotional well-being of the tenants, he found no relationship. Stubborn researcher as he is, he decided to control out for sex of tenant. He found that for women, the more mice in the apartment the better their emotional well-being, although the opposite was true for men. In this example, sex of tenant is a/an
    a. independent variable
    b. antecedent variable
    c. intervening variable
    d. suppressor variable
    e. distorter variable

DISCUSSION QUESTIONS

1. Briefly outline Stouffer's logical explanation for the anomalous finding that soldiers with more education were less resentful of being drafted than were soldiers with less education.

2. Without dealing with the four specific forms, summarize the logic of the elaboration model.

3. Compare and contrast the four specific outcomes of the elaboration model. Give an example of each that was not used in the text.

4. Explain the role of suppressor and distorter variables. Give an example of each that was not used in the text.

5. In what sense is ex post facto hypothesizing illegitimate? Why is it acceptable to formulate hypotheses after the fact in the special case of elaboration analysis?

EXERCISE 16.1

Presented below are some hypothetical data describing white college graduates: (1) whether they are scored "high" or "low" on anti-black prejudice, (2) whether they attended college in the North or in the South, and (3) whether they were raised in the North or in the South. The final column in the table indicates the number of people having the set of characteristics shown to the left. For example, the first line of the table indicates that 20 people have "high" anti-black prejudice, went to college in the North, and grew up in the North; the second line indicates that 180 people have "low" anti-black prejudice, went to college in the North, and grew up in the North.

You are to use the elaboration model to test fully the following bivariate hypothesis about the impact of region of college on anti-black prejudice:

Hypothesis: White college graduates who attended college in the South will be more prejudiced against blacks than those who attended college in the North.

In testing this hypothesis, complete the items that follow the data table.

ANTI-BLACK PREJUDICE	REGION OF COLLEGE	REGION OF CHILDHOOD	N
High	North	North	20
Low	North	North	180
High	North	South	80
Low	North	South	20
High	South	North	05
Low	South	North	45
High	South	South	160
Low	South	South	40

1. Identify the independent and dependent variables in the hypothesis. Construct the bivariate table that tests this basic hypothesis. Be sure you follow the guidelines for effective table presentation and analysis discussed in Chapter 15. Interpret the results.

2. Construct the other two bivariate tables that examine the relationship of the control variable first to the independent variable and then to the dependent variable of the original hypothesis. Interpret the results.

3. Construct the trivariate table appropriate for assessing the effect of the control variable on the original relationship. Do this by presenting two versions of the original bivariate table, one for each attribute of the control variable. Analyze the results.

4. Which form of the elaboration model **best** represents the pattern of your results? Why?

EXERCISE 16.2

This exercise resembles the preceding exercise. The variables in this case are: (1) the sex of automobile drivers, (2) whether they have driven "many" miles in their lives or "few" miles, and (3) whether they have had "many" accidents or "few" accidents.

You are to use the elaboration model to test fully the following hypothesis about the impact of sex on number of automobile accidents:

Hypothesis: Men have more automobile accidents than do women.

In testing this hypothesis, complete the items that follow the data table.

SEX	MILES DRIVEN	# OF ACCIDENTS	N
Women	Few	Many	20
Women	Few	Few	180
Women	Many	Many	80
Women	Many	Few	20
Men	Few	Many	5
Men	Few	Few	45
Men	Many	Many	160
Men	Many	Few	40

1. Identify the independent and dependent variables in the hypothesis. Construct the bivariate table that tests this basic hypothesis. Be sure you follow the guidelines for effective table presentation and analysis discussed in Chapter 15. Interpret the results.

2. Construct the other two bivariate tables that examine the relationship of the control variable first to the independent variable and then to the dependent variable of the original hypothesis. Interpret the results.

3. Construct the trivariate table appropriate for assessing the effect of the control variable on the original relationship. Do this by presenting two versions of the original bivariate table, one for each attribute of the control variable. Analyze the results.

4. Which form of the elaboration model *best* represents the pattern of your results? Why?

EXERCISE 16.3

You are to perform an elaboration analysis on one of the bivariate tables you produced and analyzed in Exercise 15.4. If you have not completed that exercise, select several independent and dependent variables from the General Social Survey codebook in Appendix 1, and use the CROSSTABS procedure to produce the bivariate tables. It will be easier to interpret the results if each of the variables you select has only a few attributes. Select a dichotomous control variable, i.e., only two attributes. (You may have to recode "don't know" responses to missing values for your control variable.)

To do the computer run, simply add another "BY" to the CROSSTABS card and follow it with your control variable. Your program should resemble the following form:

```
CROSSTABS  TABLES=VARY BY VARX BY VARZ
OPTIONS    4
```

1. Present the bivariate table that represents the original relationship between the independent variable and the dependent variable. Be sure you follow the guidelines for effective table presentation and analysis discussed in Chapter 15. Analyze the results.

2. Present the trivariate table appropriate for assessing the effect of the control variable on the original relationship. Do this by presenting two versions of the original bivariate table, one for each attribute of the control variable. Analyze the results.

3. Which form of the elaboration model *best* represents your results? Why?

EXERCISE 16.4

You are to perform another elaboration analysis on one of the bivariate tables you produced and analyzed in Exercise 15.4. You may use the same bivariate table you used in Exercise 16.3 if you wish. If you have not completed Exercise 15.4, select several independent and dependent variables from the General Social Survey codebook in Appendix 1, and use the CROSSTABS procedure to produce the bivariate tables. It will be easier to interpret the results if each of the variables you select has only a few attributes. This time select a control variable with three or four attributes.

To do the computer run, simply add another "BY" to the CROSSTABS card and follow it with your control variable. Your setup should resemble the following form:

> CROSSTABS TABLES = VARY BY VARX BY VARZ
> OPTIONS   4

1. Present the bivariate table that represents the original relationship between the independent variable and the dependent variable. Be sure you follow the guidelines for effective table presentation and analysis discussed in Chapter 15. Analyze the results.

2. Present the trivariate table appropriate for assessing the effect of the control variable on the original relationship. Do this by presenting versions of the original bivariate table for each attribute of the control variable. Analyze the results.

3. Which form of the elaboration model *best* represents your results? Why?

4. Comment on differences in analysis procedures and difficulties between this exercise (with a nondichotomous control variable) and Exercise 16.3 (with a dichotomous control variable).

Chapter 17

Social Statistics

OBJECTIVES

1. Differentiate descriptive statistics from inferential statistics.

2. Define raw-data matrix.

3. Define data reduction.

4. Define measures of association and explain the logic behind such measures, using the proportionate reduction of error principle.

5. Describe the logic and calculation of lambda, gamma, and Pearson's r.

6. Describe the relationship between levels of measurement and measures of association.

7. Briefly describe regression analysis as an analytical technique.

8. Summarize and note the utility of each of the following types of regression analysis: linear regression, multiple regression, partial regression, and curvilinear regression.

9. Summarize the cautions that should be applied when using regression analysis.

10. Define and note the utility of time-series analysis.

11. Define and note the utility of path analysis.

12. Define and note the utility of factor analysis.

13. Outline the logic, the calculation, and the interpretation of the standard error.

14. Define and state the relationship between confidence level and confidence interval and give an example.

15. List three assumptions underlying inferential statistics.

16. Define tests of significance and link this concept to that of standard error.

17. Show how the level of significance is interpreted.

18. Using the null hypothesis, describe how chi square is calculated and interpreted.

19. Summarize three dangers in interpreting the results of tests of significance.

SUMMARY

Social scientists employ two broad types of statistics. Descriptive statistics yield the capability for describing data in manageable form, and inferential statistics yield conclusions about a population from a study of a sample of that population.

Descriptive statistics serve a data reduction function. Although a raw-data matrix contains all the original information about the cases in a study, this format is very inefficient for presenting and analyzing data. Such univariate descriptive statistics as the mean, mode, and median efficiently summarize the central tendency in a frequency distribution. Measures of association perform a data reduction function by summarizing the joint frequency distributions of two variables.

Many measures of association are based on the proportionate reduction of error (PRE) principle, which incorporates a comparison between predicting a variable given its own distribution and given the joint distribution with another variable. The PRE principle is modified according to the level of measurement of the variables. Lambda is used with nominal variables, and its calculation involves using the mode. Its value ranges from zero (no association) to one (a perfect relationship). Gamma is used for ordinal variables and is based on comparing all possible pairs of cases for their relative rank ordering on both variables. The number of pairs of cases with the same ranking on the two variables is compared with the number of pairs of cases having the opposite ranking on the two variables. The values for gamma may vary from -1.0 to +1.0, thereby incorporating the direction as well as the strength of the association.

Pearson's r is used for interval and ratio level variables and uses the mean in applying the PRE principle. The use of a regression line minimizes the number of errors and yields the unexplained variation. The explained variation is the difference between the total variation and the unexplained variation. Regression analysis helps understand the Pearson's r. Regression analysis is a method by which the relationship between two or more variables can be specified in the form of a mathematical equation, known as the regression equation. This equation is a technique for representing the line that comes closest to the distribution of points in a joint frequency distribution. The general form of the equation in the case of one dependent and one independent variable is $Y = a + bX$, where X and Y represent the independent and dependent variables respectively; b represents the slope of the regression line; and a represents the Y intercept--the value of Y when X is equal to zero.

The bivariate linear regression model can be extended to the analysis of more than one independent variable, known as multiple regression analysis. This procedure allows a researcher to determine the relative contributions of each of several independent variables on a given dependent variable. Partial regression analysis resembles the elaboration model in that the equation summarizing the relationship between two variables is computed on the basis of a control variable. Curvilinear regression analysis enables the researcher to deal with relationships that fail to meet the linear model.

Caution should be applied in using regression analysis because the use of such analysis for statistical inference is based on the same assumptions made for correlational analysis: simple random sampling, the absence of nonsampling errors, and continuous interval data. Hence regression analysis can be used for interpolation (estimating cases lying between those observed) but is less useful for extrapolation (estimating cases that lie beyond the range of observations).

Path analysis is another extension of multiple regression analysis and is an efficient way to describe causal relationships among variables. It provides a graphic picture of both direct and indirect relationships among a series of independent variables as they influence a final dependent variable. This strategy requires a prior specification of the appropriate causal model by the researcher. Path coefficients are used to represent the strengths of the relationships of pairs of variables with the effects of all other variables in the model held constant.

Regression analysis may be used to analyze time-series data; such data represent changes in one or more variables over time. Such an analysis could express the long-term trend in a regression format and provide a way to test explanations for the trend. Time-lagged regression analysis enables even more sophisticated types of time-series analysis by linking changes in one variable at one point in time with changes in another variable at another point in time.

Factor analysis is somewhat different than regression analysis. It is used to discover underlying dimensions among the variations in values of several variables. Computer analysis is used to generate these dimensions, and the factor loadings provided indicate the correlation between each variable and each factor. As such, it is an excellent example of data reduction. However, factors are generated by the computer without any regard to substantive meaning, and the procedure will always generate some factors, making hypotheses useless.

Inferential statistics can be used to estimate the expected range of error involved in inferring a population value from a sample value. This statistic is known as the standard error and involves two components. The confidence level establishes how sure the researcher can be that a population value lies within a given range, the confidence interval. Several assumptions apply in inferential statistics: the sample must be drawn from the population about which inferences are being made, simple random sampling is assumed, and nonsampling errors are ignored.

Tests of statistical significance are used to specify the probability that an observed relationship between two variables (based on sample data) could be due only to sampling error. A test of statistical significance such as chi square is actually a test of the null hypothesis that there is no relationship in the population from which the sample was selected. The level of significance indicates the probability of obtaining a sample with a degree of association at least as great as that in the observed sample data from a population in which there is, in fact, no relationship.

Several dangers pertain to interpreting the results of statistical significance. First, there are no objective tests of substantive significance. Because low measures of association will be statistically significant in large samples, it is important to assess both statistical and substantive significance. Second, it is inappropriate to apply significance tests to data obtained from a total population since no sampling error occurs in such studies. Third, tests of significance are based on sampling assumptions that are frequently not met by the actual sampling design.

TERMS

1. chi square
2. confidence interval
3. confidence level
4. correlation matrix
5. curvilinear regression
6. data reduction
7. degrees of freedom
8. descriptive statistics
9. expected frequencies
10. explained variation
11. extrapolation
12. factor analysis
13. factor loadings
14. gamma
15. independence
16. inferential statistics
17. interpolation
18. joint distribution
19. lambda
20. level of significance
21. linear regression
22. measure of association
23. null hypothesis
24. path analysis
25. path coefficients
26. Pearson's r
27. proportional reduction in error
28. raw-data matrix
29. regression analysis
30. regression equation
31. regression line
32. representativeness
33. residual
34. slope
35. standard error
36. tests of significance
37. time-lagged regression analysis
38. total variation

MATCHING

____ 1. The broad type of statistics that describes data in a manageable form.

____ 2. The graphic depiction of regression analysis.

____ 3. The general type of statistic that indicates how strongly related two variables are.

____ 4. The principle on which most measures of association are based.

_____ 5. An ordinal measure of association that uses pairs as the basis of comparison.

_____ 6. A causal time-ordered model for understanding relationships.

_____ 7. A test of significance that compares observed with expected frequencies.

_____ 8. A method used to discover patterns among the variations in values of several variables.

REVIEW QUESTIONS

1. The *major* purpose of descriptive statistics is
   a. data reduction
   b. making inferences from sample to population
   c. establishing generalizability
   d. determining measures of association
   e. summarizing associations among variables

2. Professor Green wishes to employ inferential statistics. Which of the following is *not* an assumption he should keep in mind in using such statistics?
   a. samples must be drawn from the population to which he wishes to make inferences
   b. he should use simple random sampling, with replacement
   c. he should attain a 50 percent or better response rate
   d. these statistics ignore nonsampling errors
   e. all are correct assumptions

3. The proportionate reduction of error principle involves comparing
   a. errors made with expected values with errors made with observed variables
   b. percentages across categories of the independent variable
   c. errors made at the bivariate level with errors made at the multivariate level
   d. errors made on the dependent variable alone with errors made knowing both the independent and dependent variables
   e. chi square with lambda

266

4. Professor Pegret has a hunch that Capricorns are usually Jewish. To assess the relationship between zodiac sign and religion, she should use which statistic?
   a. lambda
   b. gamma
   c. chi square
   d. Pearson's *r*
   e. regression analysis

5. The regression line drawn through a scattergram plotting cases on two variables
   a. is usually not a straight line
   b. is drawn closest to the extreme values
   c. is drawn from left to right and from right to left
   d. can only be drawn if there are more than 50 cases
   e. is drawn as to minimize the deviations between each case and the line

6. Which of the following *best* represents what gamma measures?
   a. similarities and dissimilarities in rank ordering of each pair of cases on one variable
   b. a comparison of the rank order of all cases on one variable with the rank order on another variable
   c. similarities and dissimilarities in rank ordering of each pair of cases across two variables
   d. a comparison of the medians on two variables
   e. the reduction in error attained by shifting from one variable to two

7. To find out the relationship between age (in years) and frequency of movie attendance, a researcher would use which of the following statistics?
   a. chi square
   b. regression analysis
   c. Pearson's *r*
   d. lambda
   e. gamma

8. Professor George has studied the relationship between age and church attendance in a sample of 50 people. He used regression analysis. The oldest person in his sample is 58. A friend wants him to estimate the church attendance for someone who is 64. Which strategy would be best?
   a. specification

b. interpolation
c. partial regression analysis
d. extrapolation
e. multiple regression analysis

9. The *key* factor determining which measure of association to use is
   a. the size of the sample
   b. the level of measurement of the variables
   c. how many variables are involved
   d. the strength of the chi square
   e. the strength of the relationship

10. Professor Shoemaker wishes to develop an equation predicting this year's innovation rate in ten corporations based on last year's budget change and on the number of new people hired in the last two years. Which one of the following would be *best*?
    a. time-lagged regression analysis
    b. partial regression analysis
    c. quasi-experimental design
    d. time-series analysis
    e. factor analysis

11. Professor Ford has developed an index of 50 items reflecting five dimensions of the concept *love*. Which technique should she use to determine if the empirical structure among the items represents her theoretical specification of the dimensions?
    a. smallest-space analysis
    b. factor analysis
    c. multiple regression analysis
    d. partial regression analysis
    e. log-linear analysis

12. Professor Geertsen calculated a standard error of two percent in his study of support for a tuition reduction at a university, and found that 40 percent supported the motion. What is the confidence interval for the 95 percent confidence level?
    a. 36 to 44
    b. 4
    c. 38 to 43

d. 6
e. plus or minus 2

13. Which of the following is an example of the null hypothesis?
    a. there is no difference between males and females on voting
    b. there is a difference between males and females on voting
    c. males tend to vote more often than females
    d. the relationship between sex and voting is unknown
    e. all are examples of the null hypothesis

14. A student calculated a chi square significance level of .01 for a table relating sex to liberalism for 18-25 year olds. She calculated a chi square significance level of .25 for the same two variables for 26-35 year olds. Which of the following *best* summarizes the findings?
    a. she can be more sure of a real relationship between sex and liberalism among 18-25 year olds
    b. she can be relatively sure that the relationship between sex and liberalism is strong for both age groups
    c. the relationship between sex and liberalism is stronger for 18-25 year olds than 26-35 year olds
    d. the level of association between sex and liberalism is quite low for both age groups
    e. none of the above

15. Babbie's stance regarding statistical assumptions is that
    a. they should never be violated
    b. it is OK to violate them if doing so helps understand the data
    c. it is OK to violate them once you've learned a lot about statistics
    d. it is OK to violate them on very rare occasions, but you should report that you did so
    e. it is OK to violate them since the results would be the same anyway

DISCUSSION QUESTIONS

1. Compare and contrast the functions of descriptive and inferential statistics.

2. Explain the PRE principle as it relates to measures of association, and show how it applies in the case of lambda.

3. Explain how the concept of statistical significance is linked to sampling.

4. Describe what the various forms of regression analysis have in common. Then briefly differentiate among the following: linear regression, multiple regression, partial regression, curvilinear regression.

EXERCISE 17.1

Presented below are hypothetical data representing the relationship between two nominal level variables, race and political party affiliation. Select a measure of association appropriate for examining the relationship and compute it. Please show your calculations. Interpret the results.

		Race			
		White	Black	Other	Total
	Republican	70	35	10	115
Party	Democrat	20	50	40	110
	Independent	10	15	50	75
	Total	100	100	100	300

1. What measure of association did you select? Why?

2. What is the calculated value of this statistic? Show your calculations.

3. Interpret this value.

271

EXERCISE 17.2

Presented below are hypothetical data representing the relationship between two ordinal level variables, education and religiosity. Select a measure of association appropriate for examining the relationship and compute it. Please show your calculations.

		Education			
		Less than high school diploma	High school diploma	Some college or more	Total
Religiosity	Low	70	25	20	115
	Moderate	50	90	20	160
	High	20	30	60	110
	Total	140	145	100	385

1. What measure of association did you select? Why?

2. What is the calculated value of this statistic? Show your calculations.

3. Interpret this value.

EXERCISE 17.3

Calculate chi square for the data in the table in Exercise 17.1 (assume a random sample was used). Fill in the worksheet below. Cells are numbered across, not counting totals. Hence, white Republicans are cell 1, black Republicans are cell 2, and so on. A shortcut technique for calculating expected values is to multiply the column total for a cell times the row total for the same cell and divide by the total sample size.

Cell #	Observed frequency	Expected frequency	Ob - Ex	$(Ob - Ex)^2$	$\dfrac{(Ob - Ex)^2}{E}$
1					
2					
3					
4					
5					
6					
7					
8					
9					

1. What is the value of chi square?

2. How many degrees of freedom does this table have?

3. What is the level of significance for the chi square value?

4. Interpret both the chi square value and the level of significance.

EXERCISE 17.4

Exercise 15.4 involved producing several bivariate tables using the General Social Survey. Use the tables from that exercise or from Exercise 16.3 or Exercise 16.4. If you have not completed any of those exercises, select several independent and dependent variables from the codebook in Appendix 1 of this workbook and use the CROSSTABS procedure to produce the bivariate tables. Be sure to produce at least one table with both variables at the nominal level and at least one table with both variables at the ordinal level.

1. Present your table with both variables at the nominal level.

2. Interpret both chi square and lambda (or other statistics suggested by your instructor).

3. Present your table with both variables at the ordinal level.

4. Interpret both chi square and gamma (or other statistics suggested by your instructor).

EXERCISE 17.5

In this exercise you will be working with the linear regression equation:

$$Y = 3 + 1.5X$$

Use the graph provided below.

```
15

14

13

12

11

10

 9

 8

Y  7

 6

 5

 4

 3

 2

 1

 0
     0  1  2  3  4  5  6  7  8  9  10  11  12  13  14  15
                         X
```

1. Compute the estimated values of Y for each of the following values of X.

   a. $X = 3$, $Y =$

   b. $X = 2.4$, $Y =$

   c. $X = 4.6$, $Y =$

2. Plot these estimated values of Y, using the designations--A, B, C--on the graph above.

3. Identify the Y intercept (or constant) and the slope for the above line.

Part 5

The Social Context of Research

Chapter 18

The Ethics and Politics
of Social Research

OBJECTIVES

1. Discuss why ethical issues are frequently not apparent to the researcher.

2. Describe and illustrate the ethical issues involved in the following: voluntary participation, no harm to subjects, anonymity and confidentiality, the researcher's identity, and analysis and reporting.

3. Identify which of the ethical principles were violated in the Humphreys tearoom study.

4. Identify which of the ethical principles were violated in the Milgram shock study.

5. Describe two ways in which ethical and political concerns differ.

6. Summarize the link between objectivity and ideology.

7. Compare the positions on the issue that social science can (or cannot) and should (or should not) be separated from politics.

8. Illustrate how political issues exist in some of the research on race relations.

9. Identify the political issues in Project Camelot.

SUMMARY

Thus far the text has dealt with scientific and administrative constraints on practicing social research. The importance of workable compromises has been addressed. But practicing social research involves two other important considerations: ethics and politics. Social scientists often disagree on ethical and political questions because many such issues are not always immediately apparent, and few present clear and absolute solutions.

Social scientists generally agree on five basic principles in handling ethical concerns. Voluntary participation is the first principle. This principle is important because social research often represents an intrusion into people's lives and often requires that people reveal personal information about themselves. Social research often requires that people reveal such information to strangers--the researchers. Although other professionals such as physicians and lawyers also require such information and are strangers to the person, the social researcher cannot make the claim that revealing information is required to serve the personal interests of the respondent. But social scientists do argue that involvement in research may ultimately help all humanity.

Some research subjects such as students and prisoners believe that participation might benefit them personally, and in such situations the decision to participate may not be purely voluntary. A different problem is presented by the scientific norm of generalizability, which requires that research findings should be based on representative samples. Voluntary participation compromises this principle.

Social scientists should never injure participants, regardless of whether or not participants volunteered for the study. This second principle pertains primarily to psychological harm, which may result from asking people to reveal deviant behavior, unpopular attitudes, demeaning personal characteristics, and the like. This principle also applies when participants are asked to deal with aspects of themselves that they do not normally consider, a practice that may cause some agony. Subjects may also be harmed by the reporting of data, such as when recognition is possible. Increasingly, federal and other funding agencies require an independent evaluation of the treatment of human subjects, which may help the researcher identify inappropriate research strategies.

The third principle involves protecting the anonymity and confidentiality of research subjects. This principle is related to the previous one of protecting the subject from harm. A respondent is anonymous when the researcher cannot connect a given response with a given respondent. In a confidential study, the researcher is able to identify a given person's responses but promises not to reveal this identity. Confidentiality can be enhanced by using identification numbers instead of names.

Fourth, the researcher's identity can also be an ethical problem. Often it is useful and even necessary to identify oneself as a researcher. Other times it is possible and important to conceal one's research identity. Doing so may enhance the completeness and accuracy of the data collected. But doing so also involves a serious ethical dilemma since deceiving people is generally unethical. Social scientists sometimes handle this dilemma by identifying themselves as researchers but failing to inform the respondent of the true nature of the study, which also poses an ethical dilemma. It is important to debrief subjects after the study to minimize the effects of deception.

Fifth, ethical concerns enter in the analysis and reporting of data. Ethical obligations to colleagues dictate accurate reporting of the shortcomings and negative findings in a study. Also, social scientists should not identify accidental findings as the product of careful hypothesizing and theorizing.

Two studies have gained notoriety for the ethical issues they have raised: Laud Humphreys's participant observation study of homosexuality in public restrooms and Stanley Milgram's laboratory studies of obedience to authority. Humphreys's work has been attacked by people both within and outside the social scientific community for his invasion of the privacy of the homosexuals and for his deceit in obtaining their identities. Milgram's shock experiments have been criticized for the psychological suffering experienced by the participants.

Ethical issues are distinguished from political issues in two respects. The ethics of social research apply more to the methods employed, and political issues are more concerned with the substance and use of research. Second, there are no formal codes of acceptable political conduct comparable to the codes of ethical conduct that many professional associations have established.

One exception to the absence of political norms is the generally accepted stance that a researcher's personal political orientation should not influence the research completed or the interpretations of such research. This agreement enhances objectivity by means of intersubjectivity, whereby social scientists with different subjective views arrive at the same results when they apply the same techniques. However, this notion of "value-free sociology" has come under attack in recent years as Marxist and neo-Marxist researchers have argued that social science should be clearly linked to social action. They argue that explanations of the current state of affairs inevitably results in defending the status quo.

There are numerous examples of social research intertwined with politics. Social scientific research has influenced American racial policies and has generated political and ideological debates within the social science community. Project Camelot was designed to assess the causes of war and to identify the actions a government could take to preclude such wars. Many social scientists argue that such a study would involve using social scientific research to strengthen established governments and to thwart revolutionary movements. The project was canceled as the Defense Department came under increasing attack for attempting to subvert social research.

In short, social science research is closely connected with political concerns. But it is also clear that social science research proceeds even under political controversy and hostility.

TERMS

1. anonymity
2. code of ethics
3. confidentiality
4. debriefing
5. intersubjectivity
6. Project Camelot
7. value-free sociology
8. voluntary participation

MATCHING

____ 1. An ethical principle that presupposes the willingness of respondents to participate in social research.

____ 2. The condition that exists when the researcher cannot identify a given response with a given respondent.

____ 3. The condition that exists when the researcher is able to identify a given person's responses but promises not to do so publicly.

_____ 4. Published formal guidelines for conducting social research.

_____ 5. What occurs when different scientists with different subjective views can and should arrive at the same results when they employ the same research techniques.

_____ 6. Sociology that is relatively unaffected by personal values.

_____ 7. A study that showed that ultimately science is neutral on such subjects as peace and war but that individual scientists are not.

REVIEW QUESTIONS

1. Ethical considerations enter at which point in the research process?
   a. selection of topic
   b. selection of subjects
   c. data gathering
   d. data analysis
   e. at all stages

2. Ethics are *not* a consideration in which one of the following fields of research?
   a. natural sciences
   b. psychology
   c. medical
   d. sociology
   e. ethics enter in all of them

3. The *major* justification the social scientist has for requesting participation in a study is that
   a. it may help the respondent
   b. it may help all humanity
   c. it may help the social scientist
   d. it may help government officials make policy decisions
   e. it may help improve the educational system

4. The ethical principle of voluntary participation *most* threatens which scientific goal?
   a. parsimony

b. objectivity
c. cumulativeness
d. generalizability
e. intersubjectivity

5. For her senior project in political science, Cheri conducts a survey on students' attitudes and behavior concerning homosexuality. While distributing the questionnaire, she assures the group of students that no one will be able to trace responses to an individual. However, she has obtained a seating chart with the names of all the students in the class and where they were sitting. Cheri is violating which ethical principle?
   a. confidentiality
   b. anonymity
   c. harm to subjects
   d. concealed identity of researcher
   e. voluntary participation

6. The controversy surrounding Milgram's study involving "shocks" suggests he *most* violated which ethical principles?
   a. harm to subjects and concealed purpose of study
   b. anonymity and harm to subjects
   c. confidentiality and harm to subjects
   d. concealed purpose of study and anonymity
   e. concealed purpose of study and confidentiality

7. The controversy surrounding Laud Humphreys's study of homosexuals suggests he *most* violated which of the following ethical principles?
   a. anonymity and confidentiality
   b. harm to subjects and data reporting without identification
   c. concealed identity of researcher and anonymity
   d. value-free inquiry and concealed identity of researcher
   e. harm to subjects and anonymity

8. What is considered ethical is based on
   a. a list of moral absolutes
   b. the authority of the state
   c. agreed upon principles within a community
   d. cultural directives
   e. codes of political behavior

9. Federally mandated human subjects committees in universities were designed *primarily* to address which one of the following ethical principles?
   a. no harm to participants
   b. confidentiality
   c. anonymity
   d. voluntary participation
   e. identification of research purpose

10. Which of the following is *not* a difference between ethical and political aspects of social research?
    a. ethical considerations are more objective than political considerations
    b. ethical aspects include a professional code of ethics, whereas political aspects do not
    c. ethics deal more with methods, whereas political issues deal with substance
    d. ethical norms have been established, whereas political norms, for the most part, have not been established
    e. all are differences

11. Recently, Marxist scholars have argued that social research should be closely connected to social action. Which feature of science is *most* threatened by this position?
    a. intersubjectivity
    b. objectivity
    c. parsimony
    d. cumulativeness
    e. generalizability

12. The concern with Project Camelot on internal war focused on
    a. the principle of voluntary participation
    b. the principle of anonymity
    c. the role of social scientists in helping defuse revolutions
    d. the role of social scientists in helping obtain more money for defense purposes
    e. the principle of political ideology

DISCUSSION QUESTIONS

1. Summarize the ethical agreements discussed in the text. Which one do you think is the most important? Why?

2. Discuss which of the ethical agreements were violated in the Humphreys study of homosexuality and in the Milgram study of obedience.

3. Discuss the similarities and differences between the political and ethical aspects of social science research.

EXERCISE 18.1

Listed below are several of the research situations noted in the chapter as well as some others. You are to rank order these situations in terms of how seriously they violate the ethical agreements discussed in the chapter and to explain the reasons for your rankings.

a. A psychology instructor asks students in an introductory class to complete questionnaires that the instructor will analyze and use in preparing a journal article for publication.

b. After a field study of deviant behavior during a riot, law enforcement officials demand that the researcher identify those persons who were observed looting. Rather than risk arrest as an accomplice after the fact, the researcher complies.

c. After completing the final draft of a book reporting a research project, the author discovers that 25 of the 2,000 survey interviews were falsified by interviewers but chooses to ignore that fact and publish the book anyway.

d. A Ph.D. candidate gains access to an underground mine as a researcher-employee by telling management that he has a BA degree and wants to get some practical experience before going on for a degree in metallic engineering.

e. A college instructor wants to test the effect of unfair berating on exam performance. She administers an exam to both sections of a course. The overall performance of the two sections is essentially the same. The grades of one section are artificially lowered and the instructor berates the students for performing so badly. She then administers the same final exam to both sections and discovers that the performance of the unfairly berated section is worse. The hypothesis is confirmed, and the results are published.

f. In a study of sexual behavior, the investigator wants to overcome subjects' reluctance to report what they might regard as deviant behavior. To get past their reluctance, subjects are asked, "Everyone masturbates now and then; about how often do you masturbate?"

g. A researcher discovers that 85 percent of students smoke marijuana regularly at a school. Publication of this finding will probably create a furor in the community. Because no extensive analysis of drug use is planned, the researcher decides to ignore the finding and keep it quiet.

h. To test the extent to which people may try to save face by expressing attitudes on matters they are wholly uninformed about, the researcher asks for their attitudes regarding a fictitious issue.

i. A research questionnaire is circulated among students as part of their university registration packet. Although students are not told they must complete the questionnaire, the hope is that they will believe they must, thereby ensuring a higher completion rate.

j. A researcher promises participants in a study a summary of the results. Later, due to a budget cut, the summary is not sent out.

k. A professor rewrites a thesis of one of his or her graduate students into an article and lists himself/herself as the sole author.

l. A panel of reputable social scientists is pressing for Congressional approval of a National Data Service, which would combine all data on particular individuals into one master data file. The advantages of such a center would be reduced duplicity of efforts and an increased number of variables per individual.

---

1. For each of the above issues, identify what you believe to be the one or two ethical principles that are most apparent in the situation.

2. Place each situation in one of the following three groups:

Minor ethical violations	Moderate ethical violations	Severe ethical violations

3. Explain the criteria that you used in your rankings.

EXERCISE 18.2

Listed below are some goals and techniques associated with "ethical" social science research. Describe briefly how each might conflict with one or more of the "scientific" norms of social research discussed in the first few chapters. Use real or hypothetical research examples to illustrate your answers.

1. Voluntary participation

2. Anonymity and confidentiality

3. No harm to subjects

4. Identifying yourself as a researcher

5. Identifying the sponsor of your research

EXERCISE 18.3

Turn to the AAPOR Code of Ethics (Figure 18-1) presented in the chapter. Select three of the statements and describe a research situation for each in which political factors might complicate your adherence to the ethical standard.

1. AAPOR statement:

   Situation:

2. AAPOR statement:

   Situation:

3. AAPOR statement:

   Situation:

Chapter 19

The Uses of Social Research

SUMMARY

We've come full circle now. Once again, the linkages among theory, research, and statistics are highlighted. Traditional patterns of explanation die hard, particularly when reinforced by religion. Tradition and science both, however, reflect people's desire that behavior make sense and correspond with reality. Scientists use theory to help things make sense, and they use statistical analysis to assess the correspondence with reality.

People often go astray in their desire for explanations. First, they sometimes become so committed to their explanations that they ignore observable evidence. Second, they are often quite casual about their analysis of patterns in everyday life—they overrely on anecdotal evidence. Third, everyday life does not explicitly reveal the linkages between people's explanations and observations. Social scientists strive to avoid such errors by pursuing theoretical explanations that are substantiated by evidence, through research methods.

Although few of you will actually pursue jobs in social research, most will find frequent application of the skills that you have learned. Skills in sampling, survey research, observation, analysis of existing statistics, data analysis, experimentation, and evaluation research will prove useful in many occupational and avocational settings. In short, you have become a more informed consumer of research. You know the types of questions to ask about the research design, measurement, sampling, experiments, surveys, field research, analysis of existing statistics, evaluation research, data analysis, and data reporting.

Because this is an epilogue, no objectives, terms, matching questions, review questions, or discussion questions are provided. Only a few exercises follow.

EXERCISE 19.1

Find a newspaper or magazine report of some social science research and critique it. What information is missing? What is misunderstood or misstated? How accurate is the headline? Attach a copy of the report. Be sure the bibliographic information for the report is noted.

EXERCISE 19.2

Reported below is a newspaper article found in the *New York Daily News* a few years ago:

HEART DISEASE RATE HIGHER AMONG WORKING WOMEN

Married women who have children and hold clerical jobs are more likely to develop heart disease than any other group of women, according to Suzanne Haynes, Ph.D., research assistant professor at the University of North Carolina's Department of Epidemiology.

In New York this month for the Third Regional Conference of Women in Medicine, she discussed the findings from her research on cardiovascular disease.

"We followed up on some of the people who had participated in the Framingham, Mass., Heart Study," Haynes explained. Those in the 10-year study ranged from 45 to 64 years old and included 387 working women, 350 housewives and 580 men, all free of heart disease at the outset.

"We found that there was no great difference between the two groups of women. About 7% of the housewives developed heart disease after 10 years; about 8% of the working women did; and about twice that many men did.

"We concluded that it doesn't matter that much whether women work in the home or outside the home, and this finding was substantiated in three other studies.

"We also found that single working women have the lowest rate of any group; that married, widowed and divorced working women had the highest rate over the 10-year period.

"It seemed, when looking at all the different factors, that the incidence of heart disease was higher among those working women who have children; the more children, the higher the rate."

When the researchers studied the kinds of jobs held by the women in the study, it turned out that those who held clerical jobs were developing heart disease at a rate of 12%, and the rate went up proportional to the number of kids they had.

"The reasons we came up with were that this group of women had non-supportive bosses; they didn't discuss their problems with a friend or relative; and they hadn't changed jobs often. So we had to conclude that being tied to a clerical job and having a family, too, seemed to produce a high-risk situation."

Critique the report. What information is missing? What is misunderstood or misstated? How accurate is the headline? Apply the consumer's guide to social research found in the chapter.

EXERCISE 19.3

Describe a social problem that concerns you, and outline a research project you might conduct to address that problem.

EXERCISE 19.4

Describe a nonresearch situation in which you have been able to apply one or more of the concepts or techniques that you have learned in this course.

Appendix 1

General Social Survey

The General Social Survey is a survey completed annually by the National Opinion Research Center. In 1980, 1,468 persons were sampled and in 1990, 1,372 persons were sampled. Both samples were full probability samples. The samples reflect multi-stage area probability samples to the block level. The primary sampling units employed were Standard Metropolitan Statistical Areas or nonmetropolitan counties, stratified by region, age, and race before selection. The units of selection at the second stage were block groups and enumeration districts, which were stratified according to race and income before selection. The third stage of selection was that of blocks, which were selected with probabilities proportional to size.

From these complete samples, random samples of 500 per year were taken for this data set, for a total of 1,000 cases. You may wish to limit your analyses to only one year, or you may wish to do separate analyses for both years or you may wish to combine both years in one analysis. Appropriate use of the SELECT IF statement in SPSS^x (or its equivalent in other programs) with the YEAR variable will be necessary. Be very clear on which subgroups you will use in your analysis.

The first 20 variables are more often considered independent variables, and the remainder are more often considered dependent variables. However, many in the first group could be treated as dependent variables, and many in the second group could be treated as independent variables. Be sure you select an appropriate number of what you consider independent and dependent variables, or as many of each type as indicated by your instructor.

The CASE variable is a case id assigned to each person, ranging from 1 to 1,000. The RECNO variable indicates which of the two records per person contains the data for a particular variable. You must indicate which record contains the variables you have selected. Columns associated with each variable are located in parentheses under the variable name, following the record number. So, (1, 9-10) would indicate first record, columns 9-10.

CASE (1-4)	1. Case id, located in both records. 1-1,000
RECNO (6-7)	2. Record number 1 or 2 (indicated for each subsequent variable before the columns)
YEAR (1, 9-10)	3. Year of sample. 80 or 90

INCOME
(1,12-13)
	4. In which of the following groups did your total *family* income, from *all* sources, fall last year before taxes, that is?
	    1. Under $1,000
	    2. $1,000 to 2,999
	    3. $3,000 to 3,999
	    4. $4,000 to 4,999
	    5. $5,000 to 5,999
	    6. $6,000 to 6,999
	    7. $7,000 to 7,999
	    8. $8,000 to 9,999
	    9. $10,000 to 14,999
	    10. $15,000 to 19,999
	    11. $20,000 to 24,999
	    12. $25,000 or over
	    13. Refused
	    0. Missing

PRESTIGE
(1, 15-16)
	5. Hodge/Siegel/Rossi prestige scale score for respondent's occupation.
	    0. Missing
	    12-89. Prestige scale score for job

PAPRES16 (1, 18-19)	6. Hodge/Siegel/Rossi prestige scale score for father's occupation when respondent was growing up. (Same answers as PRESTIGE, #5)

MARITAL
(1, 21)

7. Are you currently—married, widowed, divorced, separated, or have you never been married?
   1. Married
   2. Widowed
   3. Divorced
   4. Separated
   5. Never married
   0. Missing

SIBS
(1, 23-24)

8. How many brothers and sisters did you have? Please count those born alive, but no longer living, as well as those alive now. Also include stepbrothers and stepsisters, and children adopted by your parents.
   0-23. Actual number
   98. Missing

ZODIAC
(1, 26-27)

9. Astrological sign of respondent.
   1. Aries   8. Scorpio
   2. Taurus   9. Sagittarius
   3. Gemini   10. Capricorn
   4. Cancer   11. Aquarius
   5. Leo   12. Pisces
   6. Virgo   0. Missing
   7. Libra

DEGREE
(1, 29)

10. Highest degree.
    0. Less than high school
    1. High School
    2. Associate/junior college
    3. Bachelor's
    4. Graduate
    7. Missing

RACE
(1, 31)

11. What race do you consider yourself?
    1. White
    2. Black
    3. Other

SEX
(1, 33)

12. Sex (coded by interviewer).
    1. Male
    2. Female

AGE
(1, 35-36)

13. Age (determined by asking date of birth).
    18-89. Actual age
    0. Missing

CHILDS
(1, 38)

14. How many children have you ever had? Please count all that were born alive at any time (including any you had from a previous marriage).
    0-7. Actual number
    8. Eight or more
    9. Missing

REGION
(1, 40)

15. Region of interview.
    1. New England
    2. Middle Atlantic
    3. East North Central
    4. West North Central
    5. South Atlantic
    6. East South Central
    7. West South Central
    8. Mountain
    9. Pacific

SIZE
(1, 42-45)

16. Size of place of interview in thousands (i.e., add three zeroes).
    0. Size less than 1,000
    1-7895. 1,000—7,895,000

POLVIEWS
(1, 47)

17. I'm going to show you a seven-point scale on which the political views that people might hold are arranged from extremely liberal—point 1—to extremely conservative—point 7. Where would you place yourself on this scale?
    1. Extremely liberal
    2. Liberal
    3. Slightly liberal
    4. Moderate, middle of the road
    5. Slightly conservative

6. Conservative
7. Extremely conservative
0. Missing

PARTYID
(1, 49)

18. Generally speaking, do you usually think of yourself as a Republican, Democrat, Independent, or what?
    0. Strong Democrat
    1. Not very strong Democrat
    2. Independent, close to Democrat
    3. Independent (neither, no response)
    4. Independent, close to Republican
    5. Not very strong Republican
    6. Strong Republican
    7. Other party, refused to say
    8. Missing

RELIG
(1, 51)

19. What is your religious preference? Is it Protestant, Catholic, Jewish, some other religion, or no religion?
    1. Protestant
    2. Catholic
    3. Jewish
    4. None
    5. Other
    8. Missing

ATTEND
(1, 53)

20. How often do you attend religious services?
    0. Never
    1. Less than once a year
    2. About once or twice a year
    3. Several times a year
    4. About once a month
    5. 2-3 times a month
    6. Nearly every week
    7. Every week
    8. Several times a week
    9. Missing

MAWORK
(1, 55)

21. Did your mother ever work for pay for as long as a year, after she was married?
    1. Yes

2. No

0. Missing

RACLIVE
(1, 57)

22. Are there any (Negroes/Blacks) living in this neighborhood now?
    1. Yes
    2. No
    0. Missing

TVHOURS
(1, 59-60)

23. On the average day, about how many hours do you personally watch television?
    0-14. Actual number hours
    -1. Missing

OWNGUN
(1, 62)

24. Do you happen to have in your home any guns or revolvers?
    1. Yes
    2. No
    3. Refused
    0. Missing

MEMNUM
(1, 64-65)

25. Number of groups or organizations to which respondent belongs.
    0-11. Actual number
    -1. Missing

FINRELA
(1, 67)

26. Compared with American families in general, would you say your family income is far below average, below average, average, above average, or far above average?
    1. Far below average
    2. Below average
    3. Average
    4. Above average
    5. Far above average
    8. Missing

We are faced with many problems in this country, none of which can be solved easily or inexpensively. I'm going to name some of these problems, and for each one I'd like you to tell me whether you think we're spending too much money on it, too little money, or about the right amount. Are we spending too much, too little, or about the right amount on. . .(applies to items 27-31)

NATENVIR
(1, 69)

27. Improving and protecting the environment?
    1. Too little
    2. About right
    3. Too much
    0. Missing

NATEDUC
(1, 71)

28. Improving the nation's education system?
    (same answers as NATENVIR, #27)

NATFARE
(1, 73)

29. Welfare?
    (same answers as NATENVIR, #27)

NATCRIME
(1, 75)

30. Halting the rising crime rate?
    (same answers as NATENVIR, #27)

NATDRUG
1, 77)

31. Dealing with drug addiction?
    (same answers as NATENVIR, #27)

CAPPUN
(2, 9)

32. Do you favor or oppose the death penalty for persons convicted of murder?
    1. Favor
    2. Oppose
    0. Missing

GRASS
(2, 11)

33. Do you think the use of marijuana should be made legal or not?
    1. Should
    2. Should not
    0. Missing

HAPPY
(2, 13)

34. Taken all together, how would you say things are these days —would you say that you are very happy, pretty happy, or not too happy?
    1. Very happy
    2. Pretty happy
    3. Not too happy
    0. Missing

SATFAM
(2, 15)

35. Tell me the number that shows how much satisfaction you get from your family life.

1. A very great deal
2. A great deal
3. Quite a bit
4. A fair amount
5. Some
6. A little
7. None
0. Missing

SATFRND
(2, 17)

36. Tell me the number that shows how much satisfaction you get from your friendships.
(same answers as SATFAM, #35)

SATJOB
(2, 19)

37. On the whole, how satisfied are you with the work you do— would you say you are very satisfied, moderately satisfied, a little dissatisfied, or very dissatisfied?
1. Very satisfied
2. Moderately satisfied
3. A little dissatisfied
4. Very dissatisfied
0. Missing

SATFIN
(2, 21)

38. We are interested in how people are getting along financially these days. So far as you and your family are concerned, would you say that you are pretty well satisfied with your present financial situation, more or less satisfied, or not satisfied at all?
1. Pretty well satisfied
2. More or less satisfied
3. Not satisfied at all
0. Missing

I am going to name some institutions in this country. As far as the *people running* these institutions are concerned, would you say you have a great deal of confidence, only some confidence, or hardly any confidence at all in them? (Applies to 39-41)

CONEDUC
(2, 23)

39. Education?
1. A great deal
2. Only some

3. Hardly any
0. Missing

CONPRESS   40. Press?
(2, 25)   (same answers as CONEDUC, #39)

CONLEGIS   41. Congress?
(2, 27)   (same answers as CONEDUC, #39)

AGED   42. As you know, many older people share a home with their
(2, 29)   grown children. Do you think this is generally a good idea or
a bad idea?
1. A good idea
2. Bad idea
3. Depends
0. Missing

The next questions are about pornography—books, movies, magazines, and photographs that show or describe sex activities. I'm going to read some opinions about the effects of looking at or reading such sexual materials. As I read each one, please tell me if you think sexual materials do or do not have that effect.

PORNRAPE   43. Sexual materials lead people to commit rape?
(2, 31)   1. Yes
2. No
0. Missing

PORNOUT   44. Sexual materials provide an outlet for bottled-up impulses?
(2, 33)   (same answers as PORNRAPE, #43)

PORNINF   45. Sexual materials provide information about sex?
(2, 35)   (same answers as PORNRAPE, #43)

Please tell me whether or not *you* think it should be possible for a pregnant woman to obtain a *legal* abortion if. . .(Applies to 46-52)

ABDEFECT   46. If there is a strong chance of serious defect in the baby?
(2, 37)   1. Yes
2. No
0. Missing

ABHEALTH
(2, 39)

47. If the woman's own health is seriously endangered by the pregnancy?
(same answer as ABDEFECT, #46)

ABNOMORE
(2, 41)

48. If she is married and does not want any more children?
(same answers as ABDEFECT, #46)

ABPOOR
(2, 43)

49. If the family has a very low income and cannot afford any more children?
(same answers as ABDEFECT, #46)

ABRAPE
(2, 45)

50. If she became pregnant as a result of rape?
(same answers as ABDEFECT, #46)

ABSINGLE
(2, 47)

51. If she is not married and does not want to marry the man?
(same answers as ABDEFECT, #46)

ABANY
(2, 49)

52. The woman wants it for any reason?
(same answers as ABDEFECT, #46)

XMOVIE
(2, 51)

53. Have you seen an X-rated movie in the last year?
1. Yes
2. No
0. Missing

HIT
(2, 53)

54. Have you ever been punched or beaten by another person?
1. Yes
2. No
0. Missing

HITOK
(2, 55)

55. Are there any situations that you can imagine in which you would approve of a man punching an adult male stranger?
1. Yes
2. No
8. Not sure
0. Missing

COURTS
(2, 57)

56. In general, do you think the courts in this area deal too harshly or not harshly enough with criminals?
1. Too harshly

2. Not harshly enough
3. About right (volunteered)
0. Missing

POSTLIFE
(2, 59)

57. Do you believe there is a life after death?
1. Yes
2. No
8. Undecided
0. Missing

HELPFUL
(2, 61)

58. Would you say that most of the time people try to be helpful, or that they are mostly just looking out for themselves?
1. Try to be helpful
2. Just look out for themselves
3. Depends (volunteered)
0. Missing

POLHITOK
(2, 63)

59. Are there any situations you can imagine in which you would approve of a policeman striking an adult male citizen?
1. Yes
2. No
0. Missing

ANOMIA5
(2, 65)

60. In spite of what some people say, the lot (situation/condition) of the average man is getting worse, not better.
1. Agree
2. Disagree
0. Missing

Appendix 2

Answers to Matching and Review Questions

Number in parentheses is the page number where answer is found.

CHAPTER 1

Matching

1.	18	(18)
2.	28	(19)
3.	4	(20)
4.	20	(22)
5.	25	(22)
6.	26	(28)
7.	30	(33)
8.	24	(34)

Review Questions

1.	d	(17)	9.	d	(25)
2.	d	(17)	10.	e	(28)
3.	b	(27)	11.	a	(32)
4.	d	(19)	12.	b	(33)
5.	c	(20)	13.	e	(34)
6.	b	(22)	14.	b	(36)
7.	d	(24)			
8.	a	(25)			

CHAPTER 2

Matching

1.	14	(46)
2.	8	(49)
3.	3	(49)
4.	1	(55)
5.	21	(55)
6.	16	(55)
7.	15	(56)
8.	5	(56)

Review Questions

1.	b	(42)	9.	a	(54)
2.	a	(45)	10.	e	(55)
3.	a	(48)	11.	b	(56)
4.	c	(53)	12.	e	(59)
5.	b	(49)	13.	b	(61)
6.	e	(53)	14.	b	(63)
7.	a	(55)			
8.	d	(54)			

CHAPTER 3

Matching

1. 4 (82)
2. 1 (78)
3. 7 (81)
4. 2 (67)
5. 6 (70)
6. 9 (71)
7. 8 (73)
8. 13 (73)

Review Questions

1. b (68)
2. b (70)
3. d (71)
4. c (71)
5. b (72)
6. e (73)
7. a (78)
8. e (81)
9. a (81)
10. c (82)
11. b (81)
12. e (77)

CHAPTER 4

Matching

1. 15 (109)
2. 7 (92)
3. 16 (92)
4. 12 (97)
5. 10 (98)
6. 4 (99)
7. 3 (99)
8. 11 (100)

Review Questions

1. c (90)
2. c (92)
3. c (90)
4. a (92)
5. d (91)
6a. a,b (93,98)
6b. b,c (93,98)
6c. d,c (94,98)
7. d (96)
8. c (97)
9. e (99)
10. d (99)
11. e (100)
12. c (101)
13. c (106)

CHAPTER 5

Matching

1. 16 (114)
2. 5 (118)
3. 13 (118)
4. 17 (122)
5. 18 (122)
6. 21 (129)
7. 25 (132)
8. 23 (117)

Review Questions

1. a (117)
2. b (118)
3. e (118)
4. a (118)
5. d (119)
6. e (120)
7. c (122)
8. b (122)
9. a (127)
10. c (132)
11. c (129)
12. c (132)
13. d (133)
14. a (133)
15. d (133)

CHAPTER 6

Matching

1.	13	(137)
2.	10	(140)
3.	11	(140)
4.	8	(141)
5.	14	(141)
6.	15	(142)
7.	3	(144)
8.	6	(148)

Review Questions

1.	c	(137)	9.	e	(148)
2.	a	(137)	10.	c	(151)
3.	d	(140)	11.	a	(151)
4.	e	(141)	12.	d	(153)
5.	c	(142)	13.	a	(154)
6.	a	(141)	14.	a	(156)
7.	d	(147)	15.	e	(159)
8.	a	(148)			

CHAPTER 7

Matching

1.	8	(167)
2.	14	(167)
3.	6	(169)
4.	19	(169)
5.	11	(178)
6.	5	(178)
7.	12	(180)
8.	18	(186)

Review Questions

1.	d	(166)	9.	e	(180)
2.	b	(166)	10	a	(181)
3.	c	(167)	11.	d	(183)
4.	b	(169)	12.	b	(183)
5.	e	(170)	13.	e	(186)
6.	c	(172)	14.	c	(187)
7.	a	(175)			
8.	c	(178)			

CHAPTER 8

Matching

1.	7	(197)
2.	15	(198)
3.	12	(199)
4.	32	(199)
5.	30	(211)
6.	36	(212)
7.	33	(215)
8.	1	(232)

Review Questions

1.	d	(197)	9.	a	(207)
2.	b	(193)	10.	a	(211)
3.	c	(197)	11.	d	(213)
4.	b	(198)	12.	c	(215)
5.	c	(198)	13.	a	(218)
6.	a	(209)	14.	e	(225)
7.	d	(204)	15.	d	(231)
8.	e	(206)			

CHAPTER 9

Matching

1.	6	(239)
2.	2	(239)
3.	28	(242)
4.	25	(244)
5.	5	(241)
6.	16	(246)
7.	8	(248)
8.	4	(248)

Review Questions

1.	e	(237)	9.	b	(245)
2.	c	(238)	10.	e	(247)
3.	a	(238)	11.	b	(247)
4.	c	(239)	12.	d	(248)
5.	a	(250)	13.	b	(249)
6.	c	(239)	14.	d	(250)
7.	c	(241)	15.	a	(255)
8.	c	(243)			

CHAPTER 10

Matching

1.	12	(262)
2.	9	(263)
3.	2	(281)
4.	7	(265)
5.	5	(275)
6.	11	(269)
7.	4	(272)
8.	8	(280)

Review Questions

1.	a	(261)	9.	d	(275)
2.	d	(263)	10.	b	(275)
3.	d	(265)	11.	a	(278)
4.	c	(266)	12.	c	(281)
5.	c	(267)			
6.	d	(269)			
7.	b	(270)			
8.	a	(273)			

CHAPTER 11

Matching

1.	9	(289)
2.	13	(292)
3.	3	(292)
4.	16	(293)
5.	14	(292)
6.	15	(301)
7.	10	(289)
8.	7	(303)

Review Questions

1.	b	(285)	9.	d	(293)
2.	a	(286)	10.	c	(297)
3.	c	(289)	11.	b	(299)
4.	a	(288)	12.	a	(301)
5.	e	(290)	13.	b	(307)
6.	b	(291)	14.	d	(308)
7.	b	(292)			
8.	c	(292)			

CHAPTER 12

Matching

1.	3	(312)
2.	10	(318)
3.	9	(318)
4.	5	(331)
5.	4	(340)
6.	11	(312)
7.	12	(340)
8.	8	(341)

Review Questions

1.	b	(313)	9.	b	(331)
2.	e	(314)	10.	c	(331)
3.	e	(317)	11.	e	(333)
4.	c	(318)	12.	d	(334)
5.	e	(318)	13.	a	(335)
6.	e	(328)	14.	a	(340)
7.	d	(329)	15.	c	(336)
8.	a	(330)			

CHAPTER 13

Matching

1.	8	(352)
2.	7	(349)
3.	6	(353)
4.	10	(365)
5.	12	(352)
6.	3	(346)
7.	1	(346)
8.	4	(349)

Review Questions

1.	e	(346)	9.	d	(352)
2.	b	(346)	10.	c	(352)
3.	c	(346)	11.	b	(353)
4.	d	(346)	12.	c	(356)
5.	b	(348)	13.	a	(358)
6.	a	(349)	14.	d	(360)
7.	e	(350)	15.	e	(366)
8.	c	(351)			

CHAPTER 14

Matching

1.	7	(382)
2.	6	(383)
3.	2	(381)
4.	8	(374)
5.	11	(385)
6.	9	(378)
7.	13	(377)
8.	12	(377)

Review Questions

1.	c	(373)	9.	e	(385)
2.	d	(374)	10.	b	(377)
3.	b	(374)			
4.	b	(375)			
5.	d	(373)			
6.	e	(383)			
7.	d	(384)			
8.	c	(385)			

CHAPTER 15

Matching

1.	16	(403)
2.	15	(390)
3.	13	(390)
4.	14	(390)
5.	19	(392)
6.	9	(389)
7.	10	(398)
8.	6	(398)

Review Questions

1.	a	(389)	9.	c	(394)
2.	e	(389)	10.	b	(397)
3.	b	(389)	11.	d	(402)
4.	d	(390)	12.	e	(403)
5.	e	(393)	13.	c	(403)
6.	a	(394)	14.	a	(404)
7.	d	(394)			
8.	b	(394)			

CHAPTER 16

Matching

1.	4	(410)
2.	2	(414)
3.	1	(414)
4.	8	(414)
5.	11	(415)
6.	7	(421)
7.	5	(416)
8.	12	(421)

Review Questions

1.	b	(410)	9.	c	(421)
2.	d	(415)	10.	d	(416)
3.	a	(415)	11.	b	(416)
4.	c	(421)	12.	e	(423)
5.	a	(415)	13.	e	(424)
6.	c	(421)	14	d	(422)
7.	e	(414)			
8.	d	(421)			

CHAPTER 17

Matching

1.	8	(430)
2.	31	(437)
3.	22	(433)
4.	27	(433)
5.	14	(434)
6.	24	(441)
7.	1	(454)
8.	12	(444)

Review Questions

1.	a	(432)	9.	b	(433)
2.	c	(448)	10.	a	(444)
3.	d	(433)	11.	b	(444)
4.	a	(434)	12.	a	(448)
5.	e	(437)	13.	a	(454)
6.	c	(434)	14.	a	(454)
7.	c	(436)	15.	b	(456)
8.	d	(440)			

CHAPTER 18

Matching

1. 8 (464)
2. 1 (467)
3. 3 (467)
4. 2 (469)
5. 5 (476)
6. 7 (477)
7. 6 (478)

Review Questions

1. e (464)
2. e (464)
3. b (465)
4. d (465)
5. b (467)
6. a (474)
7. c (471)
8. c (464)
9. a (466)
10. a (476)
11. b (476)
12. c (478)